AF879552

101 Labs CompTIA Linux+

Paul Browning, LLB (Hons), CCNP, MCSE
Arturo Norberto Baldo

https://www.101labs.net

ISBN: 978-0-9928239-2-4

Published by Reality Press Ltd.

About the Authors

Paul Browning

Paul Browning worked as a police officer in the UK for 12 years before changing careers and becoming a helpdesk technician. He passed several IT certifications and began working for Cisco Systems doing WAN support for large enterprise customers.

He started an IT consulting company in 2002 and helped to design, install, configure, and troubleshoot global networks for small to large companies. He started teaching IT courses soon after that and through his classroom courses, online training, and study guides have helped tens of thousands of people pass their IT exams and enjoy successful careers in the IT industry.

In 2006 Paul started the online IT training portal www.howtonetwork.com, which has grown to become one of the leading IT certification websites.

In 2013 Paul moved to Brisbane with his family. In his spare time he plays the guitar, reads, drinks coffee, and practices Brazilian jiu-jitsu.

Arturo Norberto Baldo

Arturo Norberto Baldo did the technical edit on this book. He is a Linux enthusiast, network engineer at AS26218 and has been a freelance IT consultant since 2012, ISOC and IETF member. He holds too many certifications to list here. He supports technologies including VMware ESXi, Vcenter, Veeam Backup And Replication, Spiceworks, osTicket, Active Directory, Windows Servers, Debian and Ubuntu Servers, Web Hosting Panels, Video surveillance systems: Bosch BVMS, Genetec, Digifort and Mileston and others.

He has worked as a network engineer, systems administrator and security specialist for several large companies. He holds a Bachelor of Technology (B.Tech.) and Master of Technology (M.Tech.). He likes to read and cycle in his spare time.

Table of Contents

Introduction–101 Labs

Welcome to your 101 Labs book.

When I started teaching IT courses back in 2002, I was shocked to discover that most training manuals were almost exclusively dedicated to theoretical knowledge. Apart from a few examples of commands to use or configuration guidelines, you were left to plough through without ever knowing how to apply what you learned to live equipment or to the real world.

Fast forward 17 years and little has changed. I still wonder how, when around 50% of your exam marks are based on hands-on skills and knowledge, most books give little or no regard to equipping you with the skills you need to both pass the exam and then make money in your chosen career as a network, security, or cloud engineer (or whichever career path you choose).

101 Labs is NOT a theory book: it's here to transform what you have learned in your study guides into valuable skills you will be using from day one on your job as a network engineer. We don't teach DHCP, for example; instead, we show you how to configure a DHCP server, which addresses you shouldn't use, and which parameters you can allocate to hosts. If the protocol isn't working, we show you what the probable cause is. Sound useful? We certainly hope so.

We choose the most relevant parts of the exam syllabus and use free software or free trials (whenever possible) to walk you through configuration and troubleshooting commands step by step. As your confidence grows, we increase the difficulty level. If you want to be an exceptional network engineer, you can make your own labs up, add other technologies, try to break them, fix them, and do it all over again.

–Paul Browning

101 LABS—COMPTIA LINUX+

This book is designed to cement the theory you have read in your Linux study guide or video training course. If you haven't studied any theory yet, then please check out our website https://www.howtonetwork.com, which also features practice exams.

The goal of this book is to dramatically improve your hands-on skills and speed, enabling you to succeed in the practical portions of the Linux+ exams and also to transfer your skills to the real world as a Linux systems engineer. We don't have space here to cover theory at all, so please refer to your Linux study guide to get a good understanding of the learning points behind each lab. Every lab is designed to cover a particular theoretical issue, such as the configuration requirements of fdisk.

If you want to become Linux+ certified, you must pass one exam:

XK0-004

The book actually shares around 60% of the content of 101 Labs—Linux LPIC1. In fact, you used to be able to pass the Linux+ and be awarded the LPIC1 but in the latest iteration, the certifications diverged with CompTIA adding several changes to the syllabus including enhanced security, troubleshooting and configuration management tools. We highly recommend taking the LPIC1 exam because you will already have done much of the hard work by the time you pass the Linux+.

We've done our best to hit every syllabus topic mentioned in the exam syllabus on the CompTIA website. Please do check the syllabus on their website which may change. Their website also gives more details on the weighting given each subject area.

It's also worth noting that once we show you how to configure a certain service or protocol a few times, we stop walking you through the steps in subsequent labs—to save valuable space. Anyway, you can always flick back a few pages to see how it's done.

We've done our best to keep the topology as simple as possible, for this reason, almost all labs have been configured on a Ubuntu installation running on a virtual machine (with internet access). Please do check out our resources page, which will cover any additional information you need: https://www.101labs.net/resources

DOING THE LABS

All of the labs are hands-on. They have been checked by several students as well as a senior Linux consultant so should be error-free. Bear in mind that each machine will differ so your output will differ from ours in many instances. If you use a distro other than Ubuntu 18.04 then your results will differ from ours significantly.

If you get stuck or things aren't working, we recommend you take a break and come back to the lab later with a clear mind. There are many Linux support forums out there where you can ask questions, and if you are a member of 101labs.net you can post on our forum, of course.

Best of luck with your studies.
–Paul Browning, CCNP, MCSE

101 LABS—LINUX+ VIDEO COURSE

Each 101 Labs book has an associated video training course. You can watch the instructor configure each lab and talk you through the entire process step by step as well as share helpful tips for the real world of IT. Each course also has 200 exam-style questions to prepare you for the real thing. It's certainly not necessary to take use this resource, but if you do, please use the coupon code '101linux' at the checkout page to get a big discount as a thank you for buying this book.

https://www.101labs.net

INSTRUCTIONS

1. Please follow the labs from start to finish. If you get stuck, do the next lab and come back to the problem lab later. There is a good chance you will work out the solution as you gain confidence and experience in configuring the software and using the commands.
2. You can take the labs in any order, but we've done our best to build up your skill level as you go along. For best results, do ALL the labs several times over before attempting the exam.
3. There are resources at www.101labs.net/resources.
4. Please DO NOT configure these labs on a live network or on equipment belonging to private companies or individuals.
5. Please DO NOT attempt to configure these labs on other Linux distros. We've chosen Ubuntu (18.04 LTS) for the labs due to the fact its the most popular Linux distribution among the top 1000 sites and gains around 500 of the top 10 million websites per day.
6. You MUST be reading or have read a Linux study guide or watched a theory video course. Apart from some configuration tips and suggestions, we don't explain much theory in this book; it's all hands-on labs.
7. It's impossible for us to give individual support to the thousands of readers of this book (sorry!), so please don't contact us for tech support. Each lab has been tested by several tech editors from beginner to expert.

ALSO FROM REALITY PRESS LTD.

Cisco CCNA Simplified
Cisco CCNA in 60 Days
IP Subnetting—Zero to Guru
101 Labs—CompTIA A+ (due 2020)
101 Labs—CompTIA Network+
101 Labs—CompTIA Linux+
101 Labs—IP Subnetting
101 Labs—Cisco CCNP
101 Labs—Cisco CCNA
101 Labs—Wireshark WCNA (due 2020)

TECHNICAL EDITORS

Thanks to all the tech editors who donated their time to check all the labs and give feedback.

Charles L. Burkholder
Carol Wood
Dante J. Alarcon
Timothy A Clark
Tim Peel
Elbert L Freeman
John DeGennaro
Steve Quan
Frank Faith
Charles Pacheco

Hardware and System Configuration

LAB 1

Boot Sequence

Lab Objective:
Learn how to manage boot options and understand the boot sequence.

Lab Purpose:
In this lab, you will practice issuing commands to the boot loader, and gain a deeper understanding of the Linux boot process, from BIOS/UEFI to completion.

Lab Tool:
Ubuntu 18.04 (or another distro of your choice)

Lab Topology:
A single Linux machine, or virtual machine

Lab Walkthrough:

Task 1:
Open the Terminal and run:

- `sudo sed -i.bak -e 's/GRUB_TIMEOUT=0/GRUB_TIMEOUT=10/' -e 's/GRUB_TIMEOUT_STYLE=hidden/GRUB_TIMEOUT_STYLE=menu/' -e 's/GRUB_CMDLINE_LINUX_DEFAULT="quiet splash"/GRUB_CMDLINE_LINUX_DEFAULT=""/' /etc/default/grub`
- `sudo update-grub`

What you're doing here is modifying the GRUB bootloader so that you can see the boot menu and various logs.

Run `dmesg | grep ATA`—you are looking for a line indicating your hard disk, beginning with something like ata2.00 or ata3.00. Make a note of this number for later.

Finally, reboot your computer or VM.

Task 2:
Upon boot, you should be greeted with a GRUB menu. Hit 'c' to enter the GRUB prompt. Here, you can run various bootloader commands. Use `ls` to explore your partitions; the format looks a bit different, for example, (hd0,msdos1). There are also commands like `lsmod`, `lspci`, and `parttool`. Do these look familiar? Run `help` for a full list.

Then, hit ESC to return to the boot menu.

Task 3:
Back at the boot menu, hit 'e' to enter a screen where you can modify the boot commands. Depending on your implementation, there may be a lot here, but you are looking for a line beginning with "linux". This is the line that loads the Linux kernel, and is the most commonly modified line for editing boot options.

At the end of that line, append `libata.force=[number]:disable`, where `[number]` is the number you noted above, such as 3.00.

Now, hit Ctrl+X to boot your computer.

Task 4:
After a couple of minutes, you may notice that something has gone wrong! You have disabled your primary hard disk, causing Linux to be unable to boot. It may have *looked* like it was booting initially, though. That's because the next step of the boot process is to load the *initial RAM disk* (initrd), prior to loading the kernel. The initrd was successful whereas the kernel step failed, which is why you should have ended up at a `(initramfs)` prompt.

In short, the Linux boot process goes like this:

1. BIOS/UEFI enumerates hardware and loads code from the configured boot device (not Linux-specific).
2. GRUB bootloader loads, parses boot commands and options.
3. Initrd is loaded, bootstraps various filesystems and modules, and then loads the kernel.
4. The init process is launched, which in turn executes all startup processes as configured within Linux.

Type `reboot` to reboot your computer/VM and return it to normalcy.

If you'd like to undo the GRUB changes made in step 1, just run:

- `sudo mv /etc/default/grub{.bak,}`
- `sudo update-grub`

Notes:

The reason an initial RAM disk is used is because Linux is a generic operating system meant to run on a wide variety of hardware and disk configurations. Having to enable checks for all of these configurations in the kernel directly would make the kernel much larger than necessary. Thus, a temporary filesystem is used to do all of the special case handling, and then load the correct modules along with the kernel.

LAB 2

Install a Boot Manager

Lab Objective:
Learn how to install and configure a boot manager.

Lab Purpose:
In this lab, you will learn about GRUB and how to configure it.

Lab Tool:
Ubuntu 18.04 (or another distro of your choice)

Lab Topology:
A single Linux machine, or virtual machine

Lab Walkthrough:

Task 1:
Classically, to edit GRUB configuration you would make changes to grub.cfg, menu.lst, and other files manually. In Ubuntu 18.04, the configurations are auto-generated based on the contents of /etc/grub.d and /etc/default/grub.

Open the Terminal, and with your favorite editor, edit /etc/default/grub:

- Change GRUB_TIMEOUT_STYLE to menu.
- Change GRUB_TIMEOUT to 10 or another value you prefer (in seconds).
- Change GRUB_CMDLINE_LINUX_DEFAULT to "", or experiment with other values for default kernel boot options.
- Change the background by setting GRUB_BACKGROUND to a beautiful image of your choice.
- (See **Answer 1** below if you're struggling to find a working /etc/default/grub file.)
- Finally, close the editor and run `sudo update-grub`

Task 2:
Have a peek at /boot/grub/grub.cfg. This is a rather long file, but you should recognize parts of it if you have done Lab 28 and customized GRUB boot commands.

If you are running this on a Linux system that's already fully installed, the next step won't be necessary. However, if you ever wish to boot a secondary disk, you might need to run `grub-install` on that disk. `grub-install` installs GRUB to a disk's *master boot record* (MBR) so that a BIOS can boot it successfully.

Task 3:
Finally, reboot your computer/VM and see/hear your shiny new GRUB boot menu. From here you may hit `e` to edit boot commands or `c` to enter a command prompt, as in Lab 28.

Answer 1:

```
GRUB_DEFAULT=0
GRUB_TIMEOUT_STYLE=menu
GRUB_TIMEOUT=10
GRUB_DISTRIBUTOR=`lsb_release -i -s 2> /dev/null || echo Debian`
GRUB_CMDLINE_LINUX_DEFAULT=""
GRUB_CMDLINE_LINUX=""
GRUB_INIT_TUNE="480 440 1"
# This file must be placed in the /boot/grub directory first
GRUB_BACKGROUND="/boot/grub/image.png"
```

Notes:
There have been multiple common bootloaders, including LILO and GRUB Legacy. GRUB2 is the most common and recommended bootloader today.

LAB 3

Kernel Modules

Lab Objective:
Learn how to install, configure, and monitor kernel modules.

Lab Purpose:
In this lab, you will learn about Linux kernel modules and how to manage them using tools such as `lsmod` and `modprobe`.

Lab Tool:
Ubuntu 18.04 (or another distro of your choice)

Lab Topology:
A single Linux machine, or virtual machine

Lab Walkthrough:

Task 1:
Open the Terminal and run `lsmod`.

This gives you a list of your currently loaded kernel modules. The left column names the module, while the right column tells you which, if any, other modules have it as a dependency.

A kernel module is an "external" part of the Linux kernel which may be optionally loaded to provide some functionality. Modules allow the kernel to support a wide variety of hardware devices and drivers without using up undue system resources.

Task 2:
Now you will remove, and reload, one of these modules. You will need to be careful which module you remove, as choosing the wrong one could render your system temporarily unusable.

Removing a sound module, such as snd_seq_midi, is safe. Run:

```
sudo rmmod snd_seq_midi
```

You may confirm that the module is removed with: `lsmod | grep snd_seq_midi`

Depending on the module you chose, this may or may not have any noticeable effect on functionality. There are many Linux kernel modules loaded on a typical system, though of course it is best not to mess with them unless you know what they do!

Reload the module with: `sudo modprobe -v snd_seq_midi`

Task 3:
You may notice that the last command in Task 2 printed a line that looked something like this:

```
insmod /lib/modules/4.18.0-21-generic/kernel/sound/core/seq/snd-seq-
midi.ko
```

`insmod` is a command used to load a single kernel module from a file, without dependency resolution. You now know the actual file name of the kernel module you just loaded (which may be different on your machine).

Now run `modinfo <file>`, where `<file>` is the filename corresponding to your chosen module. You should see a list of information, including the module's dependencies, license, and author contact information.

Task 4:
Finally, take a look at `modprobe`'s configuration files in /etc/modprobe.d. Of particular interest here is the blacklist.conf file, which blocks modules from being automatically loaded, either for troubleshooting or convenience purposes. Ubuntu 18.04 has a number of modules blacklisted by default—run `cat /etc/modprobe.d/blacklist.conf`, and read the comments to learn why.

Notes:
After updating or installing new kernel modules, you may need to run `depmod`. `depmod` is a tool to recreate the module dependency files used by `modprobe`.

LAB 4

Your Computer on the Network

Lab Objective:
Learn how to manage networking on Linux computers.

Lab Purpose:
In this lab, you will learn how to query important network configuration and gather information for connecting a Linux computer to a Local Area Network.

Lab Tool:
Ubuntu 18.04 (or another distro of your choice)

Lab Topology:
A single Linux machine, or virtual machine

Lab Walkthrough:

Task 1:
Open your Terminal and run the following commands to gather information on your current network configuration:

- `ip addr show`
- `ip route show`
- `ss -ap`
- `cat /etc/hosts`
- `cat /etc/resolv.conf`

Does your local network support IPv4, IPv6, or both?

Task 2:
Now turn off your Wi-Fi, or disconnect your Ethernet cable, or disable the network connection to your VM. Then run the first three of those commands again.

What changes occurred, and why?

Task 3:

Reconnect your network and gather some information on 101labs:

```
host -v 101labs.net
```

Can you `ping` 101labs.net? If not, how might you diagnose the problem?

Task 4:

Run `ip route show | grep default` and copy the output. You'll use it later!

Now, make sure to stop anything important you might be doing... then run: `sudo ip route del default`

Congratulations, you've just broken your internet connection by deleting the default route. You may confirm this by attempting to browse the internet with Firefox. In a real-world scenario, you could diagnose this problem by running `ip route show` and noting the lack of a default route.

To fix your connection, run: `sudo ip route add <extra>`, where `<extra>` is the output you copied earlier.

Notes:

The `net-tools` package, containing `netstat`, `ifconfig` and `route`, among other tools, is considered deprecated. Nevertheless, you may run into systems which only have these tools, and so should have a passing familiarity with them.

LAB 5

Network Configuration

Lab Objective:
Learn how to configure networking on a Linux host.

Lab Purpose:
In this lab, you will learn how to configure a Linux host as a network client, using various files and tools.

Lab Tool:
Ubuntu 18.04 (or another distro of your choice)

Lab Topology:
A single Linux machine, or virtual machine

Lab Walkthrough:

Task 1:
Open the Terminal and use `cat`, or your favorite text editor, to view the contents of the following files:

- /etc/hostname
- /etc/hosts
- /etc/resolv.conf
- /etc/nsswitch.conf

It is likely that management of these files has been swallowed up by Systemd, but it is nonetheless important to understand what each of them does (or did).

They're listed in order of decreasing simplicity. /etc/hostname simply lists your machine's hostname—in practice, to *change* the hostname, you would use `hostname` or `hostnamectl`.

/etc/hosts was DNS before DNS existed. It is a mapping of hostnames to IP addresses, useful for local addresses, small networks, and sometimes DNS servers may go here as well.

/etc/resolv.conf lists the IP addresses of your DNS servers, and possibly some other related options. (As mentioned in the file comments, this has now been taken over by `systemd-resolved`.)

/etc/nsswitch.conf is a bit outside the scope of this lab, but the relevant lines here are the ones starting with 'hosts:' and 'networks:'. The next word on those lines should be 'files', which just means that certain applications will consult the files you've just viewed when seeking that information. You may make significant edits to nsswitch.conf if you connect to centralized authentication, e.g. when an LDAP server should be queried for information rather than /etc/passwd.

Task 2:

You've worked with `ip` in previous labs to get network information, but it's worth reiterating. It is a powerful tool with a lot of uses:

- `ip address`
- `ip maddress`
- `ip route`
- `ip netconf`

Notes:

In the next lab, you will learn how to change the current IP settings, using NetworkManager.

LAB 6

Modern Tools

Lab Objective:
Learn how to troubleshoot networking issues on Linux with `iproute2`.

Lab Purpose:
In this lab, you will experiment with the latest Linux networking tools, some of which are part of the `iproute2` package.

Lab Tool:
Ubuntu 18.04 (or another distro of your choice)

Lab Topology:
A single Linux machine, or virtual machine. IPv6 must be enabled within virtual your lab for those tools to work, otherwise all steps will return a 'network is unreachable' error.

Lab Walkthrough:

Task 1:
Open your Terminal and run the following commands to gather information on your current network configuration:

- `ip addr show`
- `ip route show`
- `ss -ap`
- `hostname -f`
- `nmcli`

Task 2:

Install traceroute: `sudo apt install traceroute`

Now run a few more commands to verify that you have end-to-end connectivity with 101labs.net, and trace the routes in between.

- `ping 101labs.net`
- `traceroute 101labs.net`
- `sudo traceroute -I 101labs.net`
- `tracepath -b 101labs.net`

The first `traceroute` and `tracepath` commands here are using UDP, while the second `traceroute` is using ICMP. Sometimes the methods will yield different results; sometimes not.

If you have IPv6 connectivity, you can also experiment with those versions of the tools. (At the time of this writing, 101labs.net does not have an IPv6 address.)

- `ping6 example.com`
- `traceroute6 example.com`
- `tracepath6 -b example.com`

Notes:

For any kind of non-trivial network troubleshooting, `netcat` is a useful tool to know. It can act as an arbitrary client or server for TCP, UDP, or UNIX-domain sockets, and supports IPv4 and IPv6.

LAB 7

Legacy Tools

Lab Objective:
Learn how to troubleshoot networking issues on Linux with `net-tools`.

Lab Purpose:
In this lab, you will experiment with some classic Linux networking tools which are part of the `net-tools` package.

Lab Tool:
Ubuntu 18.04 (or another distro of your choice)

Lab Topology:
A single Linux machine, or virtual machine

Lab Walkthrough:

Task 1:
First, install the net-tools package if you don't already have it:

```
sudo apt install net-tools
```

Now run the following commands to gather information on your current network configuration:

- `ifconfig -a -v`
- `sudo netstat -tulnp`
- `route -v`
- `ipmaddr show`
- `arp -ve`

Since these tools are deprecated, it is best to uninstall them when finished: `sudo apt remove net-tools`

Notes:

The `net-tools` package has not been actively updated for about a decade. Though change is slow and it is still available in most package repos, it is clear at this point that `ifconfig` and its ilk won't be coming back. `ipmaddr` has been replaced by `ip maddress`.

LAB 8

dnsutils

Lab Objective:
Learn how to use classic Linux utilities to configure client-side DNS.

Lab Purpose:
In this lab you will work with classic tools such as `dig` to configure and troubleshoot DNS resolution.

Lab Tool:
Ubuntu 18.04 (or another distro of your choice)

Lab Topology:
A single Linux machine, or virtual machine

Lab Walkthrough:

Task 1:
In ye olden days, one could just `cat /etc/hosts /etc/resolv.conf` and gather all the DNS information one needed. This is, sadly, no longer true. Instead, run `nmcli` to find out what your current DNS servers are (see "DNS configuration" near the bottom), then save these for later. You probably have two nameservers, which will be referred to as `[dns1]` and `[dns2]` below.

Task 2:
Now you will experiment with `dig`, one of the most common and useful DNS troubleshooting utilities:

- `dig 101labs.net`
- `dig 101labs.net MX +short`
- `dig CNAME www.101labs.net [dns1]`
- `dig AAAA example.com [dns2] +short`

There are many more options available, most of which you will probably never need—but, as always, the man page is worth a skim.

Task 3:
Not to be outdone, `host` can do many of the same things that `dig` can:

- `host -v -t A 101labs.net`
- `host -t MX 101labs.net`
- `host -v -t CNAME www.101labs.net [dns1]`
- `host -t AAAA example.com [dns2]`

See the similarities?

Task 4:
By default, Ubuntu 18.04 uses a local caching nameserver. If you run a non-recursive query on this (with the dig option `+norecurse`), it will come up empty:

```
dig 101labs.net +norecurse 127.0.0.53
```

Run this on one of your main nameservers and it will work.

Notes:
`resolvconf` is a tool that was previously used in Ubuntu to manage resolv.conf. No longer installed by default, it seems to have been superseded by `systemd-resolved`.

For some users, the dig and host commands for the AAAA record required 'www' before the "example" address.

LAB 9

Filesystems and Storage

Lab Objective:
Learn about gathering information on and configuring storage devices and special filesystems.

Lab Purpose:
In this lab, you will learn about how to differentiate between various types of mass storage devices, and about sysfs, udev, and dbus.

Lab Tool:
Ubuntu 18.04 (or another distro of your choice)

Lab Topology:
A single Linux machine, or virtual machine

Lab Walkthrough:

Task 1:
Open the Terminal and run `ls /sys/block`

This will give you a list of block devices on your system. At a minimum, you should have a device such as `sda` or `xvda`. These are your standard disk devices, like hard disks and USB drives. You may also have an optical drive, such as `sr0`, and possibly one or more loopback devices.

To get more information on these devices, run `lsblk`

This will list all of those devices as well as their sizes, types, and mount points. Your hard drive(s) should be labeled as "disk", partitions as "part", loopback devices as "loop", and optical or other read-only devices as "rom".

Task 2:
Choose a device from above; for example, /dev/sda.

```
Run: udevadm info /dev/sda
```

Udev is a Linux subsystem that deals with hardware events, like plugging and unplugging a USB keyboard. Here, we are using yet another tool to gather information on a hard disk device (or another device of your choice).

Notice the first line from the output, beginning with "P:". Tying back to sysfs, this is the path for said device under the /sys filesystem. You can confirm this with `ls /sys/[path]`, where [path] is the output from the first line above.

Udev is also responsible for generating the device nodes in /dev on every boot. If you run `ls /dev`, you will see all of the devices you discovered earlier—plus many others.

Task 3:
D-Bus is a mechanism for inter-process communication (IPC). Run `dbus-monitor` and then open an application like Thunderbird. You will see a large number of messages being sent back and forth between various processes. You might need to use CTRL + C or q to quit.

Notes:
Challenge: Can you figure out how to suspend the system just by echoing a value to a file under sysfs?

LAB 10

Design Hard Disk Layout

Lab Objective:
Learn how to design a disk partitioning scheme.

Lab Purpose:
In this lab, you will learn about disk partitioning, partition types, and how to set up partitioning using tools such as `fdisk`.

WARNING: In this lab, you will begin partitioning your main disk with `fdisk`. As long as you do not use the write command, these changes will stay in memory only and your data will be safe. As an extra precaution, you may wish to run `fdisk` on a secondary drive, or create another VM just for this purpose.

Lab Tool:
Ubuntu 18.04 (or another distro of your choice)

Lab Topology:
A single Linux machine, or virtual machine

Lab Walkthrough:

Task 1:
Open the Terminal and run `sudo fdisk /dev/sda`—substitute your hard disk for /dev/sda, if sda is not the right device.

Enter `p` to see the current partition layout. If you selected your main disk, you should see at least one partition, along with its size, type, and whether it is a boot partition. For example, in the output below:

```
/dev/sda1 *      2048   41940991      41938944      20G    83      Linux
```

The disk contains a single 20GB partition, of type 83—a Linux filesystem (enter `l` to list all of the types).

Task 2:
Now let's delete (again, *from memory only*) any pre-existing partitions. Type `d` and answer the prompts until none remain.

Then:

- Enter `n` to add a new partition. This should be a primary partition, number 1, 100M in size. It would be mounted at /boot.
- Repeat this for the swap partition. Make it 4G in size, or double the system RAM. Enter `t` to change this partition type to 82 (Linux swap). Swap space is "backup RAM" which uses disk as secondary memory if your system runs out of RAM.
- Repeat this for the /var filesystem. Make it 4G in size, or whatever feels right to you based on the disk size.
- Create an extended partition that fills up the rest of the disk. Within this extended partition, you will create partitions for /home and /.
- Create a partition for the /home filesystem. Make it 4G in size, or whatever feels right to you based on the disk size.
- Repeat this for the / filesystem. It will fill up the rest of the disk.
- Enter `a` to toggle the bootable flag on partition 1.
- Enter `p` again to see what your results would be.
- **IMPORTANT:** Enter `q` to quit without writing the partition table.

In most situations, you probably wouldn't need this many partitions, and if you did, you would instead use Logical Volume Manager (LVM). LVM provides a more flexible way of managing logical volumes rather than partitions. In LVM, you would create a *volume group* consisting of one or more physical volumes (disks), and then create logical volumes on top of that in lieu of partitions.

Notes:
Some systems contain an EFI System Partition. This would show up in `fdisk` as a GPT partition, and in general should not be deleted, especially if you have a dual-booting machine.

LAB 11

Create Partitions and Filesystems

Lab Objective:
Learn how to configure disk partitions and filesystems.

Lab Purpose:
In this lab, you will learn about partitioning disks using tools such as `parted`, and creating filesystems with tools such as `mkfs`.

NOTE: `fdisk` was covered extensively in Lab 32, and so will not be covered here. It is recommended to do Lab 32 to learn more about `fdisk`.

Lab Tool:
Ubuntu 18.04 (or another distro of your choice)

Lab Topology:
A single Linux machine, or virtual machine

Lab Walkthrough:

Task 1:
The first step is to create a dummy block device to be used in the rest of the lab, so you don't erase any of your machine's actual data. Open a terminal and run:

```
dd if=/dev/zero of=block.img bs=100M count=10
```

This file is only 1GB in size. It doesn't need to be large, but if you have more space you can make it larger for more flexibility. Now run:

- `sudo losetup -fP block.img`
- `losetup -a | grep block.img | cut -d: -f1`

This should print a device name such as /dev/loop0. This is the loopback block device, and is what should be substituted everywhere you see `[dev]` for the rest of this lab.

Task 2:
Now you will partition this new block device. `gdisk` is a useful tool for creating GPT partition tables. It is based on `fdisk` and the syntax is nearly identical, so please reference Lab 32 to learn about `gdisk`. For now, use `parted` instead:

```
sudo parted [dev]
```

You can use `parted` non-interactively, but here, run the following commands in interactive mode:

- `mklabel gpt`
- `mkpart primary ext4 0 50%`
- `mkpart primary linux-swap 50% -1s`
- `quit`

These changes may prompt some warnings; they are not important for this case and you should respond in the affirmative.

It is worth noting that, unlike `fdisk` and `gdisk`, `parted` does not store all changes in memory and write them at the end, but writes every change made as you make it. Thus, it might be considered less safe than the previous two.

Task 3:
Now create an ext4 filesystem on the first partition of your block device. The name should end in "p1"—for example, if your block device is /dev/loop0, the first partition should be /dev/loop0p1: `sudo mkfs.ext4 [dev]p1`

Finally, create a swap partition as well: `sudo mkswap [dev]p2`

If you were actually setting up a new system, you would then activate the swap partition with `swapon`, but in this case you should not do that. You could also mount the `[dev]p1` partition, and start using it as a normal ext4 filesystem if you wanted to.

Task 4:
Clean up:

- `sudo losetup -d [dev]`
- `rm block.img`

Notes:
In this lab you only created an ext4 filesystem—ext4 is one of the most common filesystems used on Linux today, but it is far from the only option. Under what circumstances might you choose XFS, VFAT, exFAT, or Btrfs, instead?

LAB 12

Maintain the Integrity of Filesystems

Lab Objective:
Learn how to verify filesystem integrity and repair basic problems.

Lab Purpose:
In this lab, you will use tools such as fsck and xfs_repair to search for filesystem problems, as well as learn how to monitor free space and inodes.

Lab Tool:
Ubuntu 18.04 (or another distro of your choice)

Lab Topology:
A single Linux machine, or virtual machine

Lab Walkthrough:

Task 1:
First, set up a dummy block device for use in the rest of this lab:

- `dd if=/dev/zero of=block.img bs=100M count=10`
- `sudo losetup -fP block.img`
- `losetup -a | grep block.img | cut -d: -f1`

This should print a device name such as /dev/loop0. This is the loopback block device, and is what should be substituted everywhere you see `[dev]` for the rest of this lab (ignore all warnings you may see for parted).

Continue with:

- `sudo parted [dev] mklabel gpt`
- `sudo parted [dev] mkpart primary ext4 0 50%`
- `sudo parted [dev] "mkpart primary xfs 50% -1s"`
- `sudo mkfs.ext4 [dev]p1`

- `sudo apt -y install xfsprogs`
- `sudo mkfs.xfs [dev]p2`
- `mkdir lab57-ext4 lab57-xfs`
- `sudo mount [dev]p1 lab57-ext4`
- `sudo mount [dev]p2 lab57-xfs`
- `sudo dd if=/dev/urandom of=lab57-ext4/random bs=1M count=500`
- `sudo dd if=/dev/urandom of=lab57-xfs/random bs=1M count=500`
- `md5sum lab57-{ext4,xfs}/random`

What you've just done is created two filesystems on your block device and filled them up with a file containing random data. Then you obtained the md5 hash of each file, which you should save for later.

Task 2:

Now, you get to do something you would never do on a live system... cause damage, intentionally!

- `sudo umount [dev]p1 [dev]p2`
- `sudo dd if=/dev/urandom bs=1 count=10M of=[dev]p1 seek=1M`
- `sudo dd if=/dev/urandom bs=1 count=10M of=[dev]p2 seek=1M`

You've just caused some significant corruption to both filesystems, though unfortunately because of the nature of such corruption, the results can't be predicted. What you should do is attempt to remount both filesystems and get the MD5 sums again:

- `sudo mount [dev]p1 lab57-ext4`
- `sudo mount [dev]p2 lab57-xfs`
- `md5sum lab57-{ext4,xfs}/random`

However, it's possible that `md5sum` or even `mount` will fail for one or both filesystems. Make sure the filesystems are unmounted again, then run:

- `sudo fsck [dev]p1`
- `sudo xfs_repair [dev]p2`

You should then be able to mount the filesystems again. However, you may notice that the MD5 sums of your "important" data have been permanently altered. This is the unfortunate fact of filesystem corruption—not everything can always be saved.

Task 3:

Check disk space on both filesystems with:

- `du -hs lab57*`
- `df -h [dev]*`

Are they still full, or where one or both of your files actually deleted because of the corruption?

Task 4:

Finally, clean up:

- `sudo umount lab57*`
- `sudo losetup -d [dev]`
- `rm block.img`
- `rmdir lab57*`

Notes:

Both ext4 and XFS have advanced tuning parameters for a variety of needs. See the man pages for `tune2fs`, `xfs_fsr`, and `xfs_db`.

LAB 13

Manual Mounting

Lab Objective:
Learn how to manually mount and unmount Linux filesystems.

Lab Purpose:
In this lab, you will learn how to manually mount/unmount filesystems and how to identify filesystems via labels and UUID's.

Lab Tool:
Ubuntu 18.04 (or another distro of your choice)

Lab Topology:
A single Linux machine, or virtual machine

Lab Walkthrough:

Task 1:
Open the Terminal and run:

- `lsblk -f`
- `blkid`

These are two commands which can get you information on your block device labels and UUID's. By default your root filesystem and other filesystems may not have labels—if they do, `lsblk -f` will print those labels, which can then be passed to `blkid`.

Task 2:
Now run `mount` to identify what filesystems are currently mounted. If you have an external USB drive, you could insert that, use `lsblk -f` to identify it, and then mount/unmount it with `mount` and `umount`.

Notes:
For information about default filesystems, see the /etc/fstab file and `man fstab`.

LAB 14

Automatic Mounting

Lab Objective:

Learn how to automatically mount Linux filesystems.

Lab Purpose:

In this lab, you will learn how to automatically mount a filesystem on a Linux system at boot, using the /etc/fstab file.

Lab Tool:

Ubuntu 18.04 (or another distro of your choice)

Lab Topology:

A single Linux machine, or virtual machine

Lab Walkthrough:

Task 1:

First, you will need another filesystem to mount. This can be an external disk, or a loopback block device that you create for this purpose (see Lab 11). Identify the label or UUID of this device, then open /etc/fstab with your favorite editor. One way to identify the UUID is with `sudo lsblk -f`.

Add a line for this new device. The details will vary based on the device, but here is a template:

```
UUID=01234567-89ab-cdef-0123-456789abcdef /mnt/mydevice vfat defaults 0 2
```

The UUID for my CDROM drive (sr0) is listed below:

```
sda
└─sda1 ext4                        39584296-303a-4700-a8cd-8386f2f792cb /
sr0     iso9660   VBox_GAs_5.2.18 2018-08-14-11-58-42-18               /
media/paul/VBox_GAs_5.2.1
```

I then applied the below line to /etc/fstab:

```
UUID=2018-08-14-11-58-42-18 /media iso9660 defaults 0 2
```

When in doubt, check the man pages: `man fstab`

Save and close the file, reboot your machine, and check mounted filesystems with `mount`. If you did everything correctly, your device should be mounted!

Notes:
Users with experience in networked filesystems such as NFS may want to read about `autofs`, a tool to automatically mount filesystems as they are needed.

LAB 15

Logical Volume Manager

Lab Objective:
Learn about configuring disk space using LVM.

Lab Purpose:
In this lab, you will learn how to manage disk space in a more flexible way, by using Logical Volume Manager (LVM).

Lab Tool:
Ubuntu 18.04 (or another distro of your choice)

Lab Topology:
A single Linux machine, or virtual machine

Lab Walkthrough:

Task 1:
First, you will create two loopback volumes to use as a base for LVM to work with. See Lab 11 for more information on this, or just run these commands:

- `dd if=/dev/zero of=block.img bs=100M count=10`
- `dd if=/dev/zero of=block2.img bs=100M count=10`
- `sudo losetup -fP block.img`
- `sudo losetup -fP block2.img`
- `losetup -a | grep block | cut -d: -f1`

The last command should print two device names, such as /dev/loop0. These are your two loopback block devices, and are what should be substituted everywhere you see [`dev1`] and [`dev2`] for the rest of this lab.

Finally, install the necessary LVM tools: `sudo apt install lvm2`

Task 2:
Now you will create LVM "physical" volumes out of the two loopback devices:

- `sudo pvcreate [dev1] [dev2]`
- `sudo pvdisplay`

The second command should print a description of the two new "physical" volumes, including their names ([dev1] and [dev2]) and sizes, which should be 1GB unless you changed that in Step 1.

Task 3:
The next step is to group the two volumes into a single LVM volume group:

- `sudo vgcreate lab15 [dev1] [dev2]`
- `sudo vgdisplay`

You may be noticing a certain symmetry in these LVM commands. Once again, the first command sets up the volume group, while the second one prints information about it. Pay special attention to the "VG Name", "Cur PV" (current physical volumes), and "VG Size" fields.

Task 4:
Finally, create a couple of logical volumes from this volume group:

- `sudo lvcreate -L 1500 lab15`
- `sudo lvcreate -L 492 lab15`
- `sudo lvdisplay`

The `lvdisplay` command will show details about your two new logical volumes, including their pathnames and sizes, which you will need to know when you want to start using them. For example, to begin actually using the volumes, you would just format them (e.g. `sudo mkfs.ext4 /dev/lab15/lvol0`) and then mount (e.g. `sudo mount /dev/lab15/lvol0 /mnt`).

Task 5:
Run the following commands to undo everything and clean up the devices:

- `sudo lvremove /dev/lab15/*`
- `sudo vgremove lab15`
- `sudo pvremove [dev1] [dev2]`
- `sudo losetup -d [dev1] [dev2]`
- `rm block.img block2.img`

Notes:
There are many, many more types of configurations you can use with `lvcreate`—what you did in this lab was only the very simplest type. Give the man pages a read!

LAB 16

Linux as a Virtualization Guest

Lab Objective:
Learn how to manage Linux desktops and servers in the context of virtualization.

Lab Purpose:
If you've followed the labs in order, you are probably running this lab in a VM. In addition to desktop virtualization, with the advent of "cloud computing" and IaaS, server virtualization has become a large part of everyday life for a professional Linux administrator.

Lab Tool:
Ubuntu 18.04 (or another distro of your choice)

Lab Topology:
A single Linux virtual machine running on VirtualBox

Lab Walkthrough:

Task 1:
Open the VirtualBox Settings for the VM you are using for this lab. If possible, beef up the VM by doing the following (or if you don't have the system resources, then shrink resources assigned to the VM instead):

- Assign additional RAM and an additional processor to the VM
- Create another virtual disk image and assign it to the VM
- Assign an additional network adapter to the VM

Now reboot the VM and look to see if you can detect the additional resources. Does the memory show up in `free`? Can you see an extra processor with `lscpu`? Does `lsblk` show another disk? What about the network with `ip link show`?

The point of this exercise is to learn how easy it is to change the resources of a virtualized computer compared with a physical one. The same is true in the server world.

Task 2:
In VirtualBox, make a clone of this VM. Boot it, access the Terminal, and run:

```
ip addr show
```

Compare the results with the original VM. Are the IP address and MAC address the same, or were they automatically changed? (Depending on your settings, either could be the case.)

In a cloud scenario of multiple machines being cloned onto the same network, it is critical to make sure the network information is unique for each instance. This is also true of some security-related information, such as SSH host keys and the D-Bus machine ID.

Task 3:
Finally, it is important to understand that guest VM's must have certain features beyond a generic Linux installation to make them usable as VM's. To illustrate this, run:

```
lsmod | grep vbox
```

You may see several VirtualBox-related kernel modules, such as `vboxguest`, `vboxsf`, or `vboxvideo`, among others. Additionally, specific kernel configuration is required: `grep GUEST /boot/config*`

Notes:
Cloud-init is a package commonly used in cloud server environments to handle the unique per-server configuration on the first boot of an image deployment.

LAB 17

Timezones

Lab Objective:
Learn how to configure timezone settings.

Lab Purpose:
In this lab, you will learn how timezones work in Linux and how to configure their settings.

Lab Tool:
Ubuntu 18.04 (or another distro of your choice)

Lab Topology:
A single Linux machine, or virtual machine

Lab Walkthrough:

Task 1:
Open the Terminal and run:

- `cat /etc/timezone`
- `ls -l /etc/localtime`
- `file /usr/share/zoneinfo/$(< /etc/timezone)`

These commands just print a bit of information about your configured local timezone. /etc/timezone contains a designator, while /etc/localtime should be a symlink to a file under /usr/share/zoneinfo. As the third command shows, this is not a human-readable file, but `file` can still share some information about it.

Task 2:
Now run: `tzselect`

Going through this interactive process will, at the end, print out your timezone (which is hopefully already configured) and note how you can make it permanent for your user by setting the TZ environment variable.

Finally, use `timedatectl` to print out some additional information, and `date` to get the current time. Both commands have several more options described by their man pages.

Notes:

If your lab machine is a VM running on hardware that is often put into sleep or hibernation, you may find that your VM's RTC time has drifted. To fix this, you can enable NTP in the VM:

```
systemctl enable --now systemd-timesyncd
```

LAB 18

Locales

Lab Objective:
Learn how to configure locale settings.

Lab Purpose:
In this lab, you will learn how locales work in Linux and how to configure their settings and environment variables.

Lab Tool:
Ubuntu 18.04 (or another distro of your choice)

Lab Topology:
A single Linux machine, or virtual machine

Lab Walkthrough:

Task 1:
Open the Terminal and run: `locale`

You should see a number of variables, the first of which being LANG—as you might guess, this is the locale setting for your default language. Several other variables are listed below it, naming the settings for dates/times, phone numbers, currency, and other designations.

To see the locale settings currently supported by your system: `locale -a`

And to see supported character maps: `locale -m`

Your default locale settings are probably some variation of UTF-8, which is a standard character map on Linux.

Task 2:

If you're feeling daring (this is not recommended), you can use update-locale to change your settings to a radically different language and/or character map. For example, `sudo update-locale LANG=<setting>`

LANG=C is notable for being useful in scripting—it disables localization and uses the default language so that output is consistent.

Notes:

You can use `iconv` to convert text between character encodings.

Systems Operation and Maintenance

LAB 19

Manage Shared Libraries

Lab Objective:
Learn how to identify and install shared libraries.

Lab Purpose:
Shared libraries provide common functionality to one or more (often many more) Linux applications. In this lab, you will learn how to manage these very important libraries.

Lab Tool:
Ubuntu 18.04 (or another distro of your choice)

Lab Topology:
A single Linux machine, or virtual machine

Lab Walkthrough:

Task 1:
Open the Terminal and run:

```
cat /etc/ld.so.conf{,.d/*}
```

(The above syntax is a shortcut for "/etc/ld.so.conf /etc/ld.so.conf.d/*".)

These files are used to define shared library directories to be used by `ldconfig`. When run as root, `ldconfig` creates links and cache (used when linking a new program) to the most recent libraries in those directories, plus the "trusted" directories of /lib, /usr/lib, /lib64, and /usr/lib64.

Task 2:
Now run `ldd $(which passwd)`

This command tells you which shared libraries are linked by the `passwd` tool. The results will vary by implementation, but nearly every program should link to `libc.so.6`, among several others, at a minimum.

Occasionally, if you download software outside of a package manager, you will need to manually install its runtime shared libraries. You can use `ldd` on a binary file to figure out its dependencies, then search for those dependencies within the package manager.

Notes:

You can use the LD_LIBRARY_PATH environment variable, instead of ld.so.conf, to enable additional library directories. However, in most situations, this is not recommended.

LAB 20

Apt

Lab Objective:
Learn how to use the Apt package manager to install, upgrade, search for, and uninstall packages.

Lab Purpose:
The Apt package manager is a collection of tools meant for Debian-based distros to install and manage DEB-based packages.

Lab Tool:
Ubuntu 18.04 (or another distro of your choice)

Lab Topology:
A single Linux machine, or virtual machine

Lab Walkthrough:

Task 1:
Open the Terminal and run:

- `grep -v -e ^# -e ^$ /etc/apt/sources.list`
- `cat /etc/apt/sources.list.d/*`

These files determine which repos will be used by Apt. There are many reputable third-party repos (and many unreputable ones), which you can enable by adding to one of these files, but we'll stick with the defaults for now.

Apt uses a cache that needs to be updated periodically. Do that now with: `sudo apt update`

And then let's run all system updates: `sudo apt -y full-upgrade`

You might not have any updates, even if it's been a while since you've checked:

```
apt list --installed | grep unattended-upgrades
```

Ubuntu 18.04 should come with this package installed and configured by default.

Task 2:
Now install a useful package: `sudo apt install apt-file`

Then: `sudo apt-file update`

Now, let's say that you've downloaded the source code for some new and amazing application. Upon attempting to compile it, the code complains that "libvorbis.so" is missing. You can now use `apt-file` to see if there's a package available containing it: `apt-file search libvorbis.so`

It turns out there are several, the most relevant of which being libvorbis-dev (you can run `apt show libvorbis-dev` to confirm that that is the correct package). If you were to install that package, you would then be able to compile your application.

Notes:
You may be familiar with the classic tools such as `apt-get` and `apt-cache`. `apt` has not completely superseded those yet, but is more appropriate for interactive usage rather than scripting.

LAB 21

Dpkg

Lab Objective:
Learn how to use the dpkg package manager to install, uninstall, and obtain information on packages.

Lab Purpose:
Dpkg is a tool for installing Debian-based packages. It does not use repositories nor have automatic dependency resolution like Apt does, but it is useful for managing packages you may have downloaded outside of official repos.

Lab Tool:
Ubuntu 18.04 (or another distro of your choice)

Lab Topology:
A single Linux machine, or virtual machine

Lab Walkthrough:

Task 1:
Open the Terminal and run: `dpkg -l`

This lengthy list is, of course, your list of installed packages. To get more information on a given package, try:

- `dpkg -s sudo`
- `dpkg -L sudo`
- `dpkg -p sudo`

Some packages have configuration scripts which can be re-run with:

```
sudo dpkg-reconfigure [package]
```

To install a package manually, you would download the .deb file and run:

```
sudo dpkg -i [file]
```

Though, again, you would have to also install the dependencies manually first. To remove the package when you're done with it: `dpkg -P [package]`

Notes:

Though `dpkg` is great for information gathering, in practice it is generally better to manage your installed packages through a single central database. That may mean adding a third-party repo, or downloading a package and then manually adding it to Apt.

LAB 22

YUM

Lab Objective:
Learn how to use the YUM package manager to install, upgrade, search for, and uninstall packages.

Lab Purpose:
The YUM package manager is a collection of tools meant for RedHat-based distros to install and manage RPM-based packages.

IMPORTANT: YUM is not pre-installed with Ubuntu and it may not install correctly. In that case, we recommend setting up another VM with a RedHat-based distro, such as CentOS.

Lab Tool:
A RedHat-based distro such as CentOS. Ubuntu is not recommended for this lab.

Lab Topology:
A single Linux machine, or virtual machine

Lab Walkthrough:

Task 1:
Open the Terminal and run:

- `grep -r -v -e ^# -e ^$ /etc/yum.conf{,.d/*}`
- `cat /etc/yum.repos.d/*`

These files determine which repos will be used by YUM. There are many reputable third-party repos (and many unreputable ones), which you can enable by adding to one of these files, but we'll stick with the defaults for now.

Let's start by running all system updates: `sudo yum -y update`

If you chose Fedora, you will be using a newer tool: `sudo dnf -y update`

DNF is a newer tool which is replacing YUM in some distros. If you have one of these distros, you can safely replace all instances of `yum` with `dnf` in this lab.

Task 2:

Let's say that you've downloaded the source code for some new and amazing application. Upon attempting to compile it, the code complains that "libvorbis.so" is missing. You can look to see if there's a package available containing it: `yum provides */libvorbis.so`

It turns out there are several, the most relevant of which being libvorbis-devel (you can run `yum info libvorbis-devel` to confirm that that is the correct package). If you were to install that package with `sudo yum -y install libvorbis-devel`, you would then be able to compile your application.

Notes:

To experiment with a third major package manager, called Zypper, it is suggested to use a third distro, called OpenSUSE. This is outside the scope of this lab, but if you use Zypper after using Apt and YUM you will likely find that the commands and syntax are quite familiar.

LAB 23

RPM

Lab Objective:
Learn how to use the RPM package manager to install, uninstall, and obtain information on packages.

Lab Purpose:
RPM is a tool for installing RPM-based packages. It does not use repositories nor have automatic dependency resolution like YUM does, but it is useful for managing packages you may have downloaded outside of official repos.

IMPORTANT: RPM is not pre-installed with Ubuntu and it may not install correctly. In that case, we recommend setting up another VM with a RedHat-based distro, such as CentOS.

Lab Tool:
A RedHat-based distro such as CentOS. Ubuntu is not recommended for this lab.

Lab Topology:
A single Linux machine, or virtual machine

Lab Walkthrough:

Task 1:
Open the Terminal and run: `rpm -qa`

This lengthy list is, of course, your list of installed packages. To get more information on a given package, try:

- `rpm -qs sudo`
- `rpm -q --dump sudo`

To install a package manually, you would run: `sudo rpm -i [file]`, where `[file]` can be either a downloaded .rpm or a URL. Again, though, you would have to also install the dependencies manually first. To remove the package when you're done with it: `rpm -e [package]`

Task 2:

Another useful tool is `rpm2cpio`. This tool converts a .rpm file into a cpio archive and spits it out on stdout. This makes it easy to access the files within, independent of RPM. For example:

```
rpm2cpio package.rpm | cpio -dium
```

Notes:

Though `rpm` is great for information gathering, in practice it is generally better to manage your installed packages through a single central database. That may mean adding a third-party repo, or downloading a package and then manually adding it to YUM/DNF.

LAB 24

Creating Users and Groups

Lab Objective:
Learn how to create and customize users and groups.

Lab Purpose:
In this lab, you will learn how to create users and groups, as well as set their passwords.

Lab Tool:
Ubuntu 18.04 (or another distro of your choice)

Lab Topology:
A single Linux machine, or virtual machine

Lab Walkthrough:

Task 1:
Open the Terminal and run:

```
sudo sh -c 'echo "Hello World" > /etc/skel/hello.txt'
```

Here, you are adding a file to the /etc/skel directory, which determines the default files in a new user's home directory.

Now:

- `sudo useradd -m foo`
- `sudo cat ~foo/hello.txt`

You should see the output "Hello World". What happened is that you created a new user, called foo (using the `-m` switch to ensure a home directory was created). Every file in /etc/skel was then copied to the new user's home directory.

Finally, set an initial password for this user with: `sudo passwd foo`

Task 2:
Now let's add a system user. Run: `sudo useradd -r bar`

When adding a system user, `useradd` does not add any account or password aging information, and sets a user ID appropriate for a system user (typically below 1000). It also does not create a home directory unless you specify `-m`.

Task 3:
Now let's create a group and add our new users to it:

- `sudo groupadd baz`
- `sudo usermod -a -G baz foo`
- `sudo usermod -a -G baz bar`

Verify that the users were added with: `grep ^baz /etc/group`

Task 4:
Finally, clean up:

- `sudo rm /etc/skel/hello.txt`
- `sudo userdel foo`
- `sudo userdel bar`
- `sudo groupdel baz`
- `sudo rm -r /home/foo`

Notes:
`usermod` is a very useful command for managing users. In addition to adding and removing users from groups, it allows you to manage account/password expirations and other security features.

LAB 25

User Profiles

Lab Objective:
Learn about global and user profiles.

Lab Purpose:
In this lab, you will manage shell profiles and learn which files can be used to customize both global profiles and those for specific users.

Lab Tool:
Ubuntu 18.04 (or another distro of your choice)

Lab Topology:
A single Linux machine, or virtual machine

Lab Walkthrough:

Task 1:
Open your favorite editor via the terminal, and take a look at the following files (some of these files may not exist, that's normal):

- /etc/profile
- /etc/skel/.bash_profile and/or ~/.bash_profile
- /etc/skel/.bash_login and/or ~/.bash_login
- /etc/skel/.profile and/or ~/.profile
- /etc/bash.bashrc
- /etc/skel/.bashrc and/or ~/.bashrc
- /etc/skel/.bash_logout and/or ~/.bash_logout

Bash attempts to read the first four files (in preference order) every time you start a *login* shell, while it reads the latter two whenever you start an *interactive* shell. Typically, a login shell is started once per boot, or once per SSH login, while an interactive shell is started every time you open the Terminal application (or a new tab within it)—but, as with all things, there are exceptions. Finally, Bash reads ~/.bash_logout when a login shell is exited.

You won't necessarily understand everything that's happening in these files right away. The key takeaway is that this is where you can make permanent changes to every aspect of a shell's profile, including environment variables, shell options, and even text and background colors.

Task 2:
Test this theory by adding a simple welcome message. Open ~/.bashrc in your favorite editor and add the following line at the end of the file:

```
echo "Welcome, $USER! You've successfully modified the .bashrc file!"
```

Save and quit, exit the terminal, then open a new terminal, and you should be greeted with your message.

Note that this only applies to your user. If you wanted it to apply to a different user, you would have to modify that user's own .bashrc file. To apply it to all future users, you would edit /etc/skel/.bashrc, or /etc/bash.bashrc to apply it to all *current* (and future) users.

Notes:
An interesting environment variable to experiment with is PS1. Running `echo $PS1` will print out a confusing mess of special symbols, but simply running `PS1="$ "` will make it immediately apparent that this, in fact, what defines your prompt!

LAB 26

Users

Lab Objective:
Learn how to add, modify, and remove users.

Lab Purpose:
In this lab, you will learn about the different types of Linux users and a few tools to add, modify, and remove them.

Lab Tool:
Ubuntu 18.04 (or another distro of your choice)

Lab Topology:
A single Linux machine, or virtual machine

Lab Walkthrough:

Task 1:
Open the Terminal and run: `cat /etc/passwd`

This file is an inventory of all users on your system. The passwd file is a database with seven fields, separated by colons:

1. Username
2. Encrypted password (in practice, hardly ever used—see below)
3. User ID
4. Group ID
5. Comment
6. Home directory
7. Default shell

Take note of the *root* user, which should be listed on the first line. This is the administrative user, and is the only user that can unconditionally do anything on the system. By running a command preceded with `sudo`, you are running that command as the root user. (You can also use `sudo -i` or `su` to access a root shell directly.)

If you look at the user ID's, you will notice that most of them, on a default system, are below 1000. These are *system* users, typically used to run specific services, rather than running those as root, which can create security problems. On most systems, human user ID's begin at 1000 or 500.

You can easily see the passwd information for your own user with: `grep ^$USER /etc/passwd`

Task 2:
Now run: `sudo cat /etc/shadow`

The shadow file is a sensitive database containing hashed user passwords, among other information. Be careful with the contents of this file! It contains nine fields, again, separated by colons—however, on a default Ubuntu install, only the first three are likely to be significant:

1. Username
2. Encrypted password
3. Date of last password change

The other fields contain information like account expiration dates and minimum/maximum password ages, which are not configured on a default system. See `man 5 shadow` for more information.

You can see this information for your own user with: `sudo grep ^$USER /etc/shadow`

Task 3:
Now run:

```
sudo sh -c 'echo "Hello World" > /etc/skel/hello.txt'
```

Here, you are adding a file to the /etc/skel directory, which determines the default files in a new user's home directory.

Now:

- `sudo useradd -m foo`
- `sudo cat ~foo/hello.txt`

You should see the output "Hello World". What happened is that you created a new user, called foo (using the `-m` switch to ensure a home directory was created). Every file in /etc/skel was then copied to the new user's home directory.

Finally, set an initial password for this user with: `sudo passwd foo`

Task 4:
Finally, clean up:

- `sudo rm /etc/skel/hello.txt`
- `sudo userdel foo`
- `sudo rm -r /home/foo`

Notes:
`usermod` is a very useful command for managing users. In addition to adding and removing users from groups, it allows you to manage account/password expirations and other security features. `usermod` will be discussed in the next two labs.

LAB 27

Groups

Lab Objective:
Learn how to add, modify, and remove groups.

Lab Purpose:
In this lab, you will learn about Linux groups and a few tools to add, modify, and remove them.

Lab Tool:
Ubuntu 18.04 (or another distro of your choice)

Lab Topology:
A single Linux machine, or virtual machine

Lab Walkthrough:

Task 1:
Open the Terminal and run: `cat /etc/group`

As you might expect, this is a database of all groups on the system. It contains four fields separated by colons:

- Group name
- Encrypted group password
- Group ID
- List of users who are members

Run `groups` to learn which groups your user has membership in. You can get more information, including group ID's, with the `id` command.

Task 2:

Now let's create a group and add ourselves to it:

- `sudo groupadd foo`
- `sudo usermod -a -G foo $USER`

Verify that your user was added with: `grep ^foo /etc/group`

Task 3:

You can use groupmod to change properties of the group, like its name:

- `sudo groupmod -n bar foo`
- `grep ^bar /etc/group`

Finally, clean up with `sudo groupdel bar`

Notes:

Several directives in /etc/login.defs will affect the behavior of `groupadd` and `groupmod`. See the man pages for `groupadd`, `groupmod`, and login.defs for more information.

LAB 28

Pipes and Redirection

Lab Objective:
Learn how to use pipes and redirect input and output in Bash.

Lab Purpose:
Bash has two commonly-used features, known as pipes and I/O redirection, that make life easier when using Linux. In this lab, you will learn how to make use of these powerful features.

Lab Tool:
Ubuntu 18.04 (or another distro of your choice)

Lab Topology:
A single Linux machine, or virtual machine

Lab Walkthrough:

Task 1:
Open the Terminal application and run:

```
mkdir lab13
cd lab13
echo "hello world" > hello
cat hello
```

You just *redirected* the output from your `echo` command into the hello file. The `>` is a shortcut; the proper version of this would be `1>`, where `1` is called a *file descriptor*, which references the *standard output*.

Task 2:
Now run:

```
ls nonexistent 2>> hello
cat hello
```

Based on the new contents of the hello file ("ls: cannot access 'nonexistent': No such file or directory"), what can you surmise about the function of `2>>`? Here, `2` is a file descriptor for *standard error.*

Task 3:

Sometimes, you want to redirect both output *and* error to the same place. In ye olden days, you would have to do something ugly like this: `ls foo > bar 2>&1`

However, modern versions of Bash have an easy-to-use shortcut: `ls foo &> bar`

Task 4:

We've talked about redirecting output, but what about input? To learn about that, run the following commands:

```
cat < hello

read foo <<< "foo"
echo $foo

cat << END-OF-FILE > goodbye
hello
goodbye
END-OF-FILE
cat goodbye
```

In short: `<` redirects input from a file name, `<<` starts a here document, and `<<<` redirects input from another command.

Task 5:

Pipes (`|`) let you use the output of a command as the input to another command. In many situations (but not all), `|` and `<<<` are kind of a reverse of one another. For example, the output of...

```
echo "hello world" | grep e
```

... is identical to the output of...

```
grep e <<< "hello world"
```

Try to predict the output of the following command string before you run it (see **Answer 1** below):

```
grep non hello | cut -d: -f3
```

Task 6:

Finally, clean up:

```
cd ~
rm -r lab13
```

Answer 1:

```
No such file or directory
```

Notes:

`grep` searches for matching patterns in a string, while `cut` splits the input into pieces. Both are very common tools that you will use more in subsequent labs.

LAB 29

Process Text Streams Using Filters

Lab Objective:
Learn how to use small text filtering programs to obtain command output.

Lab Purpose:
In this lab, you will send text files and output through a number of utility commands.

Lab Tool:
Ubuntu 18.04 (or another distro of your choice)

Lab Topology:
A single Linux machine, or virtual machine

Lab Walkthrough:

Task 1:
Open the Terminal and run:

```
echo "foo
BAR
Baz
Quux123
456plugh
7xy8zz9y0
Hello
goodbyE" | nl -n ln > lab29.txt
```

Here, you are creating a simple text file—when piped through `nl`, the file is created with line numbers. Use `cat` and `less` to check the file's contents.

Task 2:
`head` and `tail` are useful for obtaining only the first or last n lines of a file:

- `head -3 lab29.txt`
- `tail -3 lab29.txt`

Task 3:
Now you will get *hashes* of this file. Hashing uses one-way algorithms to verify the integrity of files (or passwords); if the hashes of two files match, then those files are theoretically identical. Get the MD5, SHA256, and SHA512 hashes, respectively:

- `md5sum lab29.txt`
- `sha256sum lab29.txt`
- `sha512sum lab29.txt`

The output from those three commands should be, respectively:

```
e18bce7fb26d0394587e6692106c99b3  lab29.txt
970468127af90d4e4eed6fd7e85461bcf02ac49910959fccb2179c2bc5e41d87
lab29.txt
9fd0c523be2951ecd683e53b79feceecb804aaa31bdf2906b5458268794ff5f85bbd2f
6ecdd944bb68693d65ac39c23c69438d23b43d3060f413aa240c13a629  lab29.txt
```

If your hashes don't match, you may have a typo!

Task 4:
`cut` is a useful tool to obtain only the fields you want from structured flat files. For example, compare the difference in output between these two commands:

- `cut -f1 lab29.txt`
- `cut -f2 lab29.txt`

The first command lists the line numbers, while the second lists only the words.

You can use `sort` to sort the output in various ways; for example, by reversing it:

```
sort -r lab29.txt
```

There's also a command called `uniq` which can ignore or count duplicate instances of some line or field. (`sort` also has the `-u` switch to do this in a single step).

Sometimes, you may also need to obtain a byte-level representation of a file in octal or other format. This can be useful if a file contains characters which are not readable by your terminal:

```
od lab29.txt
```

Finally, use `wc` to count characters, words, and lines:

- `wc -c lab29.txt`
- `wc -w lab29.txt`
- `wc -l lab29.txt`

Did you get 109, 16, and 8, respectively?

Task 5:
Now you will use the `tr` filter to modify the output and replace all digits with underscores:

```
cat lab29.txt | tr [0-9] _
```

`sed` is another more complicated, but more featureful, way of accomplishing this same task:

```
sed 's/[0-9]/_/g' lab29.txt
```

A full discussion of `sed` syntax is outside the scope of this lab, but it can do far more than `tr` alone and is a tool well worth learning.

Finally, split this file into four more files of two lines each:

- `split -l2 lab29.txt lab29`
- `ls lab42*`
- `cat lab42aa`

Task 6:
Now clean up with: `rm lab29*`

Notes:
In addition to `cat`, you can also view the contents of compressed files directly. Use `zcat`, `bzcat`, or `xzcat`, for gzipped, bzipped, or LZMA formats, respectively.

LAB 30

Find and Globbing

Lab Objective:
Learn how to use advanced filename expansion in Bash, as well as the `find` command to locate and act on specific files.

Lab Purpose:
In this lab, you will learn about shell globbing, and how to use the `find` command to locate files based on type, size, etc. and execute commands on those files.

Lab Tool:
Ubuntu 18.04 (or another distro of your choice)

Lab Topology:
A single Linux machine, or virtual machine

Lab Walkthrough:

Task 1:
It is important to understand that, although shell globbing shares some commonalities with regular expressions, Bash itself does not recognize the full regex syntax. Instead, Bash simply recognizes and expands wild cards.

Open the Terminal and run:

- `mkdir lab44`
- `cd lab44`
- `touch a1 a2 a12 b1 b2 b12 c1 c2 c12`

Task 2:
To understand how advanced globbing works, run the following commands and observe the output (on the right):

- `ls a?`   `a1   a2`
- `ls a*`   `a1   a12   a2`

- `ls [ab]?` a1 a2 b1 b2
- `ls [ab]*` a1 a12 a2 b1 b12 b2
- `ls [^ab]*` c1 c12 c2
- `ls ?[1-2]` a1 a2 b1 b2 c1 c2
- `ls ?[1-2]*` a1 a12 a2 b1 b12 b2 c1 c12 c2

Task 3:
Now, apply this shell globbing to find and execute a command on a certain set of files (copy and paste won't work for the below):

```
find . -name "c?" -execdir ls -l {} \;
```

What this command is doing is searching in the current directory (recursively) for all files named "c?", which in this case matches c1 and c2. It then effectively executes `ls -l [file]` on each file found. The `{}` syntax references the filename, while the escaped semicolon denotes the end of arguments to the `ls` command.

Experiment further with `find`:

- `sudo find / -not -type l -perm -o+w`
- `sudo find / -perm -u+s -user root -type f`

Both of the above commands are useful for security auditing purposes. The first one searches for (non-symlink) world-writable files. The second one searches for files which are "setuid root," or in other words, run with root permissions by a non-root user.

Task 4:
Clean up:

- `cd ..`
- `rm -r lab44`

Notes:
Another useful command is `file`, which tells you a given file's type. Can you figure out how to use `file` in combination with find to locate all text files within your home directory?

LAB 31

Redirection and File Descriptors

Lab Objective:

Learn how to redirect input and output in Bash.

Lab Purpose:

Bash has a commonly-used feature, known as I/O redirection, that makes life easier when using Linux. In this lab, you will learn how to make use of this powerful feature.

Lab Tool:

Ubuntu 18.04 (or another distro of your choice)

Lab Topology:

A single Linux machine, or virtual machine

Lab Walkthrough:

Task 1:

Open the Terminal application and run:

```
mkdir lab46
cd lab46
echo "hello world" > hello
cat hello
```

You just *redirected* the output from your `echo` command into the hello file. The `>` is a shortcut; the proper version of this would be `1>`, where `1` is called a *file descriptor*, which references the *standard output*.

Task 2:

Now run:

```
ls nonexistent 2>> hello
cat hello
```

Based on the new contents of the hello file ("ls: cannot access 'nonexistent': No such file or directory"), what can you surmise about the function of `2>>`? Here, `2` is a file descriptor for *standard error.*

Task 3:
Sometimes, you want to redirect both output *and* error to the same place. In ye olden days, you would have to do something ugly like this: `ls foo > bar 2>&1`

However, modern versions of Bash have an easy-to-use shortcut: `ls foo &> bar`

Task 4:
We've talked about redirecting output, but what about input? To learn about that, run the following commands:

```
cat < hello

read foo <<< "foo"
echo $foo

cat << END-OF-FILE > goodbye
hello
goodbye
END-OF-FILE
cat goodbye
```

In short: `<` redirects input from a file name, `<<` starts a here document, and `<<<` redirects input from another command.

Task 5:
You can also create your own file descriptors. Observe:

- `exec 3<> foo`
- `echo "Hello World" >&3`
- `cat foo`
- `exec 3>&-`
- `echo "fail" >&3`

What this is doing is opening file descriptor 3 (for both reading and writing), with the file foo, and sending output to that. The fourth line then closes the file descriptor, causing the last `echo` command to fail.

Task 6:

Finally, clean up:

```
cd ~
rm -r lab46
```

Notes:

To open a file descriptor for reading only, you could use `exec 3< file`, or for writing only, `exec 3> file`.

LAB 32

Pipes

Lab Objective:
Learn how to use pipes in Bash to use the output of one command as the input of another.

Lab Purpose:
Bash has a commonly-used feature, known as pipes, that makes life easier when using Linux. In this lab, you will learn how to make use of this powerful feature.

Lab Tool:
Ubuntu 18.04 (or another distro of your choice)

Lab Topology:
A single Linux machine, or virtual machine

Lab Walkthrough:

Task 1:
Pipes (|) let you use the output of a command as the input to another command. In many situations (but not all), | and <<< are kind of a reverse of one another. For example, the output of...

```
echo "hello
world" | grep e
```

... is identical to the output of...

```
grep e <<< "hello
world"
```

Try to predict the output of the following command string before you run it (see **Answer 1** below):

```
grep non hello | cut -d: -f3
```

Task 2:

In Lab 46, you learned how to redirect command output. Now run:

```
echo "Hello World" | tee hello
cat hello
```

What's going on here? The `tee` command redirects output to a file while also sending it to stdout. You can use a special `|&` pipe to redirect both stdout and stderr:

```
rm hello
ls hello |& tee hello
cat hello
```

`tee` also has a `-a` switch to append to the file rather than overwriting it.

Task 3:

While a pipe passes the output of a command as the input of another command, `xargs` passes the output of a command as the *argument(s)* of another command:

```
echo hello | xargs cat
rm hello
```

The `xargs` man page describes a number of useful arguments, including setting a delimiter and forcing interactive prompting for each argument.

Answer 1:

```
No such file or directory
```

Notes:

Challenge: Chain together a series of commands that uses each of: pipes, `ls`, `xargs`, and at least one redirection.

LAB 33

vi Navigation

Lab Objective:
Learn how to open, close, and navigate the `vi` editor.

Lab Purpose:
In this lab, you will learn about one of the classic (but often opaque to new users) Linux text editors, `vi`.

Lab Tool:
Ubuntu 18.04 (or another distro of your choice)

Lab Topology:
A single Linux machine, or virtual machine

Lab Walkthrough:

Task 1:
Open the Terminal and run `vi /etc/passwd`. Assuming you've not run this as root, `vi` should tell you at the bottom that the file is read-only. That's fine, since you won't be making any changes right now. Instead, explore just navigating `vi`:

- Use the h, j, k, and l keys, or the arrow keys, to navigate the cursor between characters and lines.
- Enter /username, or ?username, to search forward and backward, respectively, for your username. Use n or N to hop to the next/previous match, respectively.
- Enter 10G to hop to line 10. Then just enter G to hop to the bottom of the file.
- Finally, type :q to quit. Or if you've somehow accidentally made changes, type :q! to force quit without saving them. If you are in insert mode press Esc first and then : when the cursor appears in the bottom left you can press q!

Notes:
The EDITOR environment variable defines which editor is used by programs that ask for one, such as `sudoedit`. By default this may be set to `nano`. If you're comfortable enough with `vi`, you may want to change this variable.

LAB 34

vi Modes

Lab Objective:

Learn how to use modes within the `vi` editor.

Lab Purpose:

In this lab, you will learn about one of the classic (but often opaque to new users) Linux text editors, `vi`.

Lab Tool:

Ubuntu 18.04 (or another distro of your choice)

Lab Topology:

A single Linux machine, or virtual machine

Lab Walkthrough:

Task 1:

Open the Terminal and run `vi lab55.txt`. Now, explore the modes of `vi`:

- Type i to enter insertion mode, and enter a few lines of text. Type ESC to leave this mode.
- Navigate to the middle of a line and type a to enter insertion mode one character after the cursor's position. Enter more text or hit ESC to exit the mode.
- Navigate to the middle of a line and type I to insert text at the beginning of this line. Hit ESC to exit insertion mode.
- Type A to add text at the end of the current line. Again, hit ESC to exit.
- Navigate to a line and type o to add a line of text below it. Hit ESC to exit insertion mode.
- Type O to add a line of text above the line where your cursor is. Again, hit ESC to exit.
- Use y to copy ("yank") text; for example, y$ to yank from the cursor to the end of a line, or yy to yank the whole line. Then, press p to paste.

- Use d to delete text; for example, d$ to delete from the cursor to the end of a line, or dd to delete the whole line. Type x a few times to delete a few characters under the cursor.
- Finally, use :q! to quit, or if you've written something useful, :w! to save it. You may also use :wq!, :x, or ZZ to save and quit.

Notes:

Hopefully, you can see that there is symmetry among `vi` commands—a/A, o/O, y/yy and d/dd, etc. Now that you're a `vi` pro, install and try its improved version, `vim`!

LAB 35

Create and Change Hard and Symbolic Links

Lab Objective:
Learn how to create and manage hard links and symbolic links.

Lab Purpose:
In this lab, you will work with hard links, symbolic (soft) links, and learn the difference between copying and linking.

Lab Tool:
Ubuntu 18.04 (or another distro of your choice)

Lab Topology:
A single Linux machine, or virtual machine

Lab Walkthrough:

Task 1:
Open the Terminal and run:

- `touch foo`
- `ln -sv foo myfoo`
- `ls -l myfoo`
- `echo hello > foo`
- `cat myfoo`
- `rm myfoo`
- `ls -l foo`

What just happened? You created a *symbolic link* to a file (foo) called myfoo. The `ls` output shows this link. A symbolic link is simply a reference to an existing file. This way, you may have multiple references to a single file—edit the original file, and all of the references instantly update, as shown by `cat`.

When you remove the link, the original file still remains. (If you remove the original file while keeping the symlink, you will have what's called a *broken link*, just like on the internet.) This is useful for some system configurations.

Task 2:

Now run:

- `ln -v foo myfoo`
- `echo goodbye > foo`
- `cat myfoo`
- `rm foo`
- `ls -l myfoo`
- `cat myfoo`

You just created a different type of link, called a *hard link*. Hard links behave similarly to symlinks in the sense that when the original is modified the links follow, and vice versa. However, a hard link keeps its data if the original file is deleted. Hard links also cannot be made across filesystem or partition boundaries, and directories cannot be hard-linked.

Task 3:

Finally, clean up with `rm myfoo`

Notes:

Under the hood, hard links are really acting upon *inodes*. A hard link creates another file pointing to the same inode as the original file. (Symlinks work at a higher level, pointing directly to a file or directory name.) You can see the inode number with `ls -i`, or see how many hard links share a given file's inode in the second column of `ls -l`

LAB 36

SysVInit and Systemd

Lab Objective:
Learn how to manage SysVInit and Systemd, and understand the differences between them.

Lab Purpose:
SysVInit and Systemd are two different ways of managing Linux startup processes. SysVInit is considered the "classic" method, while Systemd has supplanted it in many distros today.

Lab Tool:
Ubuntu 18.04 (or another distro of your choice)

Lab Topology:
A single Linux machine, or virtual machine

Lab Walkthrough:

Task 1:
Ubuntu 18.04 is one of the distros that has switched to Systemd. However, many SysVInit-based scripts are still present and active:

```
ls /etc/init.d
```

Every file in this directory is a script which starts, stops, checks status, and possibly other features for a given service. You can see which scripts are enabled for which *runlevels* with:

```
ls -lR /etc/rc*
```

Take a look at the symlinks listed under /etc/rc5.d. Runlevel 5 is the default boot runlevel, when you're booting normally into a desktop with display manager. Runlevel 0 (under /etc/rc0.d) contains links to the scripts run when your computer is halted.

Task 2:
Now run:

```
systemctl list-unit-files --state=enabled
```

These are the services which are enabled at boot within Systemd, and should be mostly distinct from the ones listed under /etc/rc*. Use CTRL + C or q to quit.

While SysVInit relies on standard shell scripts, Systemd uses *unit files* with its own custom format. As just one example, take a look at:

```
cat /lib/systemd/system/rsyslog.service
```

Systemd unit files can have many options. See `man systemd.unit` for more information.

Task 3:
Finally, take a look at those system logs with:

```
journalctl -xe
```

Journalctl is Systemd's replacement for the classic syslog. Again, however, Ubuntu still has quite a few logs in classic text format—see /var/log.

Notes:
Ubuntu once used Upstart as a replacement for SysVInit. However, that project is currently in maintenance mode and no longer being updated. Ubuntu has migrated to Systemd as a replacement for Upstart.

LAB 37

Runlevels and Boot Targets

Lab Objective:
Learn how to set and change Linux runlevels and boot targets.

Lab Purpose:
The standard Linux *runlevels* are as follows:

- 0: Halt
- 1 (or S): Single-user mode
- 2: Multi-user mode, no networking
- 3: Multi-user mode, with networking
- 4: Unused, or runlevel 3 + display manager
- 5: Unused, or runlevel 3 + display manager
- 6: Reboot

Lab Tool:
Ubuntu 18.04 (or another distro of your choice)

Lab Topology:
A single Linux machine, or virtual machine

Lab Walkthrough:

Task 1:
Make sure all of your work is saved. Then, you will enter single-user mode (rescue mode) from the Terminal:

```
sudo telinit 1
```

You will be greeted with a root command prompt—this is the original Linux! As hinted by the name, this mode is typically used for rescue operations. If you ever forget your root password (and the root partition isn't encrypted), this is how you could reset it.

From here, type `reboot` to reboot your machine into a GRUB menu. (See Lab 1 if you cannot see the GRUB boot menu.)

Task 2:

From the GRUB boot menu, type 'e' to edit the boot commands. Append `3` to the line beginning with "linux", then hit Ctrl+X to boot.

You should find yourself prompted to log in via the command line, rather than the graphical prompt you may be used to. After logging in, you will have a shell just as if you had opened the Terminal application.

Now run `sudo telinit 5` to start the display manager.

You may also use `init` for the same purpose.

Notes:

It should be noted that, according to the `telinit` man page in Ubuntu 18.04, "the concept of SysV runlevels is obsolete". In the past, you could also use /etc/inittab to set the default runlevel—this is also removed in Ubuntu 18.04.

LAB 38

Systemd and Processes

Lab Objective:
Learn how to manage Systemd and properly shutdown/restart services.

Lab Purpose:
In this lab you will practice managing running services with Systemd and gracefully stopping and starting processes.

Lab Tool:
Ubuntu 18.04 (or another distro of your choice)

Lab Topology:
A single Linux machine, or virtual machine

Lab Walkthrough:

Task 1:
Open the Terminal and run:

```
systemctl status rsyslog
```

You should receive some basic status output showing that the rsyslog service is, indeed, running.

Now: `sudo systemctl restart rsyslog`

Check the logs again and you will see the rsyslog startup messages from just a moment ago.

Task 2:

Run: `ls /lib/systemd/system`

These are the Systemd unit files (there are a lot). As the equivalent to SysV runlevels, these unit files are symlinked from various *targets* in /etc/systemd/system. Run:

- `ls -l /etc/systemd/system`
- `ls -l /etc/systemd/system/multi-user.target.wants`

Task 3:

Acpid is an ACPI daemon for managing hardware events, like sleep or hitting the power button. To check whether ACPI is active on your system (it probably is):

```
acpi_available && echo yes || echo no
```

If yes, then you can run `acpi_listen` and hit the power or sleep buttons, or close the screen, to trigger and view ACPI events.

Notes:

A classic command is called `wall`, which was used to notify users of system maintenance and other events. In practice, it is rarely used anymore, but still present on most Linux systems.

LAB 39

Foreground and Background Jobs

Lab Objective:
Learn how to run jobs in the foreground and background.

Lab Purpose:
Sometimes, you want to run a process in Linux and then walk away, or hide the job in the background so you don't see it. In this lab, you will learn how to do that.

Lab Tool:
Ubuntu 18.04 (or another distro of your choice)

Lab Topology:
A single Linux machine, or virtual machine

Lab Walkthrough:

Task 1:
Open the Terminal and run `sleep 10000`, then press Ctrl+Z. Now run:

- `jobs`
- `bg`
- `jobs`
- `fg`

Hit Ctrl+C to cancel the sleep job.

When you first ran the `sleep` command and then pressed Ctrl+Z, that command was *stopped* (although the term "stopped" may be misleading—"paused" is more accurate). When stopped, a job is no longer running, ticking down seconds, or whatever it's supposed to be doing. The `bg` command changes that, making the job run in the background. You can see the list of running jobs with `jobs`, and bring the most recent background job into the foreground with `fg`. Note that you can run `fg` on stopped jobs as well, you don't have to start them running first.

To run a task in the background directly, simply append a `&`, like: `sleep 10000 &`

Task 2:
Run `sleep 10000 &`, then exit your terminal completely by closing the window (do not use the `exit` command).

When you open a new terminal, run `ps -ef | grep sleep` and you should find that your sleep process has terminated. To keep a job running even after closing a shell session, run the command under `nohup`:

```
nohup sleep 10000 &
```

If you exit the terminal now and come back, you will still find that process running. `nohup` causes a command to ignore what's called the *hangup* signal.

Task 3:
At times, you may need to run a normal foreground process, but still have it running even after you have walked away. This is more common on servers, where an admin will connect via OpenSSH and wants to decouple a running process from their own shell, while still monitoring for problems.

There are two tools, screen and tmux, which can help with this, but on a default setup you'll need to install them first: `sudo apt -y install screen tmux`

`screen` and `tmux` operate slightly differently, but the principles are the same. Start with `screen`:

- `screen`
- `i=0; while true; do i=$(($i+1)); echo $i; sleep 1; done`

Now hit Ctrl+A, followed by D. These keystrokes will detach from your `screen` session and return to your shell. You can view these sessions with `screen -list`. Now:

- `tmux`
- `j=0; while true; do j=$(($j+1)); echo $j; sleep 1; done`

Now hit Ctrl+B, followed by D. Again, this will detach from the session and put you back at the shell, but your process is still running. You view these sessions with `tmux ls`.

Finally, return to each session, respectively, with `screen -x` and `tmux attach`. (Hit Ctrl+C and run `exit` in between them to terminate the processes.) If there is more than one session, you will be prompted to choose one, otherwise the command will reattach to the running session.

Notes:

`screen` and `tmux` have a variety of options, comparable to text editors in some respects. Neither of them is "better," but you might want to explore both tools and decide which you prefer.

LAB 40

Cron

Lab Objective:
Learn how to use cron utilities to schedule automated system tasks.

Lab Purpose:
In this lab, you will manage automated system tasks using the classic `cron` utilities.

Lab Tool:
Ubuntu 18.04 (or another distro of your choice)

Lab Topology:
A single Linux machine, or virtual machine

Lab Walkthrough:

Task 1:
Open the Terminal and run: `cat /etc/crontab`

In this file, you will likely see a few rows of commands to be run at certain times. The first five columns designate the minute, hour, day-of-month, month, and day-of-year, respectively, for a given job to be run. Then you will see the user (usually root) and, finally, the actual command. See `man 5 crontab` for a full description of crontab format.

On a default Ubuntu installation, /etc/crontab should contain "meta" commands to run cron jobs from other files—/etc/cron.hourly, /etc/cron.daily, and so forth. Look at these next:

```
ls /etc/cron.{hourly,daily,weekly,monthly,d}
```

As you might guess, these directories hold jobs to be run hourly, daily, weekly, monthly, or on some other interval. Inspect a few files to see what jobs are run periodically on your system.

On some systems, a user-based crontab is used. In this case, run `crontab -l` and `sudo crontab -l` to view the jobs. These jobs are stored in /var/spool/cron/crontabs.

Task 2:

Run `crontab -e` and add a cron job for your user:

```
* * * * * date > ~/foo
```

Then: `sleep 60 && cat ~/foo`

You should see that your cron job has run (every minute) and printed the date into file foo. Clean up with `crontab -e`, delete the line you added, and `rm foo`

Notes:

/etc/cron.allow and /etc/cron.deny control user access to `crontab`. On a default Ubuntu system, these files may not exist—according to the man page, that means only root should have access to `crontab`, but default system configuration allows *all* users access. See `man crontab` to understand how these files work.

LAB 41

At and Systemd

Lab Objective:
Learn how to use `at` and Systemd utilities to schedule automated system tasks.

Lab Purpose:
In this lab, you will manage automated system tasks with Systemd and scheduled tasks using `at`.

Lab Tool:
Ubuntu 18.04 (or another distro of your choice)

Lab Topology:
A single Linux machine, or virtual machine

Lab Walkthrough:

Task 1:
Open the Terminal and run: `sudo apt install at`

In contrast to `cron`, `at` is used for running one-time jobs at some time in the future.

Now run:

- `echo "touch foo" | at now + 1 min`
- `atq`
- `sleep 60 && ls foo`
- `rm foo`

You scheduled a `touch foo` command to be run in the future; `atq` shows this job (which you could delete if you wanted to, using `atrm`). One small caveat, though—`at` will not necessarily schedule your job *exactly* one minute in the future, when used with this syntax. The seconds are truncated, so, in fact, it may run less than one second from "now". `at` isn't generally used in scenarios requiring such precision!

Like with cron, `at` can be user-restricted in the /etc/at.allow and /etc/at.deny files. In Ubuntu, by default, a blacklist is set up—see this with `cat /etc/at.deny`

Task 2:

Any Systemd service can be configured with a timer, which can use an OnCalendar directive to mimic `cron`, for example:

```
...
[Timer]
OnCalendar=*-*-* 03:30:00
Persistent=true
...
```

See `man systemd.timer` for more info.

You can also create transient timer units, a la `at`, with `systemd-run`:

```
systemd-run --on-active=60 touch ~/foo
```

That will touch a file after 60 seconds. This can also be used with pre-existing services, for example, if you have a unit called *myunit*:

```
systemd-run --on-active="12h" --unit myunit.service
```

Notes:

Though Systemd can effectively replace both `cron` and `at`, it is not without problems. Cron-like jobs especially take far more time to set up within Systemd, compared to adding a single line to a crontab file.

LAB 42

Manage Printers and Printing

Lab Objective:
Learn how to manage print jobs using CUPS.

Lab Purpose:
In this lab, you will learn about managing print queues and jobs using CUPS and the LPD compatibility interface.

Lab Tool:
Ubuntu 18.04 (or another distro of your choice)

Lab Topology:
A single Linux machine, or virtual machine

Lab Walkthrough:

Task 1:
To eliminate variability around printer hardware and all the problems it brings (and in case you don't have a printer handy), this lab will assume printing to a PDF file instead. If you would like to print to a real printer, ignore this step. Otherwise, run: `sudo apt install printer-driver-cups-pdf` (you may have to run 'apt-get update --fix-missing' in order to install cups-pdf correctly.

Verify with `lpstat -t`—you should see "device for PDF: cups-pdf:/" as part of the output. Or, if you plug in a real printer, it should be auto-detected. (If not, then it would be easier to print to PDF for the purposes of this lab.)

Finally, check where your files should be printed: `grep ^Out /etc/cups/cups-pdf.conf`

You may see something like ${HOME}/PDF as the directory where your "printed" files will end up. You can change this if you like; if you do, finalize it with `sudo systemctl restart cups`

Task 2:

You can probably guess what happens next:

- `echo "Hello World" | lpr`
- Locate the file in the directory you identified above (it may have an odd name, like stdin___tu_PDF-job_1.pdf), and open it in a PDF viewer or web browser.

You should find a nondescript PDF file with your text printed in the top left corner. If you didn't change anything, this should be under PDF/ in your home directory.

Task 3:

Now some other helpful commands:

- `lpr -T gibberish`
- Type some gibberish, followed by Ctrl+C to cancel. (The `-T` flag also influences the filename after printing.)
- `lpq`
- The previous command should tell you the job number (third column) of the queued job. Then run: `lprm [number]`
- You canceled the job (if you do it quickly enough—there is a timeout), but it will still show up as "completed" via `lpstat -W completed`

Notes:

`lpadmin` can be used to add and configure printers which are not auto-detected. For example, you would add a cups-pdf printer manually with:

```
sudo lpadmin -p cups-pdf -v cups-pdf:/ -E -P /usr/share/ppd/cups-pdf/
CUPS-PDF_opt.ppd
```

LAB 43

Processes and Configuration

Lab Objective:
Learn how to manage running processes and program configurations.

Lab Purpose:
In this lab, you will learn how to configure various system processes and how to manage and monitor those processes while they are running.

Lab Tool:
Ubuntu 18.04 (or another distro of your choice)

Lab Topology:
A single Linux machine, or virtual machine

Lab Walkthrough:

Task 1:
Open the Terminal and run `ls /boot`

The contents will vary, but generally what you will see is a Linux kernel file (name starting with `vmlinuz`), initrd file, System.map, a `grub` configuration directory, and sometimes a copy of the kernel configuration.

Everything in this directory, including the `grub` config file (`/boot/grub/grub.cfg`), is related—as you might expect—to your system boot processes. This is one directory you don't want to mess with unless you know what you're doing!

Task 2:
Next, run: `ls /etc`

In Linux parlance, 'etc' stands for 'editable text configuration.' `/etc` is the primary directory tree for all system configuration; with few exceptions, nearly all configurations are stored in, or linked from, `/etc`.

The few (non-user-specific) exceptions might be in `/dev`, `/sys` or `/proc`. These are special, dynamically-generated filesystems. You may occasionally read information from these filesystems, but most of the time you shouldn't be writing directly to them.

Task 3:
Run the following commands in your Terminal:

- `free -m`
- `ps -ef`
- `top        # press q to quit`

These are three common tools to monitor processes and their resource usage. (Got a runaway process that won't quit via the normal means? Try `kill` or `pkill`.)

Notes:
`/dev` contains special files called device nodes, which are linked to device drivers. `/sys` and `/proc` contain files by which the kernel presents non-process and process-related information, respectively. (In reality, this is more muddled, but that is the ideal separation.)

LAB 44

PCI Devices and Peripherals

Lab Objective:
Learn about gathering information on and configuring PCI devices and peripherals.

Lab Purpose:
In this lab, you will use tools such as `lsusb` and `lspci` to determine hardware resources and manipulate USB and PCI devices.

Lab Tool:
Ubuntu 18.04 (or another distro of your choice)

Lab Topology:
A single Linux machine, or virtual machine

Lab Walkthrough:

Task 1:
Open the Terminal and run:

```
for dev in $(ls /sys/bus/usb/devices/*/product); do echo -n "$dev :";
cat $dev; done
```

The output will be a list of USB devices connected to your system, such as the following:

```
/sys/bus/usb/devices/1-1/product: USB Tablet
/sys/bus/usb/devices/usb1/product: OHCI PCI host controller
```

What we're interested in is the USB bus and port from the first field. In this example, there are two devices, a USB tablet at 1-1 and a PCI controller at usb1.

You may also use `lsusb` to gather more information on these devices.

Task 2:
You will now **optionally** disable and re-enable one of the above USB devices. This is optional because if done incorrectly, it could render your system temporarily unusable until a reboot.

Let's say that you have a webcam at 1-1.6. This is safe to disable. You would run:

```
sudo sh -c 'echo 1.1-6 > /sys/bus/usb/drivers/usb/unbind'
```

Test the device you disabled to confirm that it is no longer available. To re-enable the device, simply run:

```
sudo sh -c 'echo 1.1-6 > /sys/bus/usb/drivers/usb/bind'
```

Task 3:
Run: `lspci -v`

This is a list of your PCI devices. Take note of the devices which list kernel modules, on the last line beginning with "Kernel modules". You can confirm that these modules are loaded by getting a list of the currently loaded kernel modules with `lsmod`

Now you will remove, and reload, one of these modules. As in the previous step, you need to be careful which module you remove, as choosing the wrong one could render your system temporarily unusable.

Removing a sound module, such as snd_seq_midi, is safe. Run:

```
sudo modprobe -r snd_seq_midi
```

You may confirm that the module is removed with: `lsmod | grep snd_seq_midi`

Depending on the module you chose, this may or may not have any noticeable effect on functionality. There are many Linux kernel modules loaded on a typical system, though of course it best not to mess with them unless you know what they do!

Reload the module with: `sudo modprobe snd_seq_midi`

Notes:
It is good to understand the /proc and /sys filesystems—all information on USB and PCI devices is stored there, if you know where to look. The next lab will dive into these filesystems.

LAB 45

Install and Configure X11

Lab Objective:
Learn about the X11 window system and how to configure it.

Lab Purpose:
In this lab, you will explore various aspects of X11 configuration.

Lab Tool:
Ubuntu 18.04 (or another distro of your choice), and a running X11 system. If you aren't sure whether your system runs X11, test with `sudo ps -ef | egrep -i x11\|xorg`

Lab Topology:
A single Linux machine, or virtual machine

Lab Walkthrough:

Task 1:
Open the Terminal and attempt to look at /etc/X11/xorg.conf or /etc/X11/xorg.conf.d. These paths may not exist—on a default Ubuntu 18.04 VM install, they don't. If not, run blah and take a look there instead—for example, in /usr/share/X11/xorg.conf.d. You are just trying to view some example Xorg config files.

A typical X11 config will have one or more sections, each section dealing with a single device; for example, a monitor, or a graphics card, or an input device. Within a section, a given device may have several directives, like specifying a driver or various options for the device.

If you are setting up Xorg on a new server, you can run `Xorg -configure` to generate a new configuration. This is not recommended on a machine of any importance, as it is easy to mess up. (Though a backup should be automatically created.)

Task 2:

Now run:

- `echo $DISPLAY`
- `xhost`
- `xauth list`

These commands will print your Xorg display number, authorized hosts, and authorization entries, respectively. In nearly all cases, the first output should be `:0`, and the second output should be something like `SI:localuser:ubuntu`. The only situation in which this would be radically different is if your machine was used as a remote X server, and especially if you were connected to X remotely. (In practice, this is rare—most Linux professionals manage remote servers via SSH only.) The third output lists authorization entries, or "magic cookies", for each display.

Notes:

Wayland is a newer windowing system that aims to replace X11. Ubuntu used Wayland as default in version 17.10, but moved back to X11 in 18.04 due to bugs. It is worth understanding both Wayland and X11.

LAB 46

Accessibility

Lab Objective:
Learn how to configure accessibility features within Linux.

Lab Purpose:
In this lab, you will examine various accessibility settings on a Linux desktop.

Lab Tool:
Ubuntu 18.04 (or another distro of your choice)

Lab Topology:
A single Linux machine, or virtual machine

Lab Walkthrough:

Task 1:
Open the Settings application, then click Universal Access in the left sidebar.

Experiment with the following settings:

- High Contrast
- Large Text
- Cursor Size
- Zoom
- Screen Reader
- Screen Keyboard
- Repeat Keys
- Mouse Keys (see the menu in the upper right after selecting this option)

Notes:
Some accessibility features require specific hardware. For example, gestures are obviously more meaningful on a touch-screen device or with an external drawing tablet.

Security

LAB 47

Basic Security and Identifying User Types

Lab Objective:
Learn how to identify the differences between the root user, standard users, and system users.

Lab Purpose:
In this lab, you will learn about the different types of Linux users and a few tools to identify and audit them.

Lab Tool:
Ubuntu 18.04 (or another distro of your choice)

Lab Topology:
A single Linux machine, or virtual machine

Lab Walkthrough:

Task 1:
Open the Terminal and run: `cat /etc/passwd`

This file is an inventory of all users on your system. The passwd file is a database with seven fields, separated by colons:

1. Username
2. Encrypted password (in practice, hardly ever used—see below)
3. User ID
4. Group ID
5. Comment
6. Home directory
7. Default shell

Take note of the *root* user, which should be listed on the first line. This is the administrative user, and is the only user that can unconditionally do anything on the system. By running a command preceded with `sudo`, you are running that command as the root user. (You can also use `sudo -i` or `su` to access a root shell directly.)

If you look at the user ID's, you will notice that most of them, on a default system, are below 1000. These are *system* users, typically used to run specific services, rather than running those as root, which can create security problems. On most systems, human user ID's begin at 1000 or 500.

You can easily see the passwd information for your own user with: `grep ^$USER /etc/passwd`

Task 2:
Now run: `sudo cat /etc/shadow`

The shadow file is a sensitive database containing hashed user passwords, among other information. Be careful with the contents of this file! It contains nine fields, again, separated by colons—however, on a default Ubuntu install, only the first three are likely to be significant:

1. Username
2. Encrypted password
3. Date of last password change

The other fields contain information like account expiration dates and minimum/maximum password ages, which are not configured on a default system. See `man 5 shadow` for more information.

You can see this information for your own user with: `sudo grep ^$USER /etc/shadow`

Task 3:
Now run: `cat /etc/group`

As you might expect, this is a database of all groups on the system. It contains four fields separated by colons:

1. Group name
2. Encrypted group password
3. Group ID
4. List of users who are members

Run `groups` to learn which groups your user has membership in. You can get more information, including group ID's, with the `id` command.

Task 4:

Finally, a few commands you can use to audit user logins:

- `who`
- `w`
- `last`
- `last $USER      # For your own user`

Notes:

In the next lab, you will learn how to add regular users and system users. In practice, you will rarely need to add system users manually—these are typically added along with the services that use them.

LAB 48

Managing File Permissions and Ownership

Lab Objective:
Learn how to manipulate file permissions and ownership settings.

Lab Purpose:
In this lab, you will learn to use `chmod` and `chown`, as well as view permissions and ownership settings with `ls`.

Lab Tool:
Ubuntu 18.04 (or another distro of your choice)

Lab Topology:
A single Linux machine, or virtual machine

Lab Walkthrough:

Task 1:
Open the Terminal and run (you may need to add the user 'foo' if you removed it on the last lab):

- `echo "Hello World" > foo`
- `ls -l foo`

Look at the first field; you should see `-rw-r--r--`

This indicates the user, group, and other permissions. The last nine characters, in groups of three, denote these permissions. In this instance:

- `rw-` indicates read/write (but not execute) permissions for the user who owns the file
- `r--` indicates read-only permissions for the group that owns the file
- `r--` indicates read-only permissions for all non-owners, a.k.a. "world"

The first character indicates the type of file. In this case, it is a regular file; directories begin with `d`.

Who are the user and group owners of this file? The third and fourth fields of `ls -l` tell us that. By default, it should be your own user and primary group.

Task 2:
Now run:

- `sudo chown root foo`
- `ls -l foo`
- `cat foo`

You've just changed the user ownership to root, while keeping the group ownership. As the file has group- and world-read permissions, you can still see its contents.

Task 3:
Now run:

- `sudo chmod o-r foo`
- `ls -l foo`
- `cat foo`

That `chmod` command removes read permissions from other. However, as you still have group ownership, you can still see the file's contents.

Task 4:
Now run:

- `sudo chmod 600 foo`
- `ls -l foo`
- `cat foo`

This `chmod` command sets the permissions explicitly, to read-write for the owning user only. As that is root, we can no longer read the file.

Task 5:
Finally, clean up with `sudo rm foo`

Notes:
Execute permissions come into play on executable files as well as directories. If a user/group cannot "execute" a directory, it cannot view the contents of said directory or any subdirectories.

LAB 49

Special Directories and Files

Lab Objective:
Learn how to use temporary files and directories, symbolic links, and special permissions.

Lab Purpose:
In this lab, you will work with symbolic links, special file/directory permissions, and temporary files and directories.

Lab Tool:
Ubuntu 18.04 (or another distro of your choice)

Lab Topology:
A single Linux machine, or virtual machine

Lab Walkthrough:

Task 1:
Open the Terminal and run: `ls -ld /tmp`

Notice the permissions: `drwxrwxrwt`

The `t` at the end indicates what is called the *sticky bit*. This means that only users/groups who own a given file may modify it. This is important on world-writable directories, such as those holding temporary files, to prevent users from messing with other users' files.

Task 2:
Now run:

- `ln -sv $(mktemp) mytmp`
- `ls -l mytmp`
- `rm mytmp`

What just happened? `mktemp` created a randomly-named temporary file. Then you created a *symbolic link* to that file called mytmp. The `ls` output shows this link. A symbolic link is simply a reference to an existing file. This way, you may have multiple references to a single file—edit the original file, and all of the references instantly update. This is useful for some system configurations.

Notes:

In addition to /tmp, there is also /var/tmp, which is typically used for larger and/or longer-lasting temporary files. /tmp is usually cleaned on every reboot; the same is not necessarily true for /var/tmp.

LAB 50

File Permissions

Lab Objective:
Learn how to manipulate permissions and ownership settings of files.

Lab Purpose:
In this lab, you will learn to use `chmod`, `chown`, and `chgrp`, as well as `umask`.

Lab Tool:
Ubuntu 18.04 (or another distro of your choice)

Lab Topology:
A single Linux machine, or virtual machine

Lab Walkthrough:

Task 1:
Open the Terminal and run:

- `echo "Hello World" > foo`
- `ls -l foo`

Look at the first field; you should see `-rw-r--r--`

This indicates the user, group, and other permissions. The last nine characters, in groups of three, denote these permissions. In this instance:

- `rw-` indicates read/write (but not execute) permissions for the user who owns the file
- `r--` indicates read-only permissions for the group that owns the file
- `r--` indicates read-only permissions for all non-owners, a.k.a. "world"

The first character indicates the type of file. In this case it is a regular file; directories begin with `d`.

Who are the user and group owners of this file? The third and fourth fields of `ls -l` tell us that. By default, it should be your own user and primary group.

Task 2:
Now run:

- `sudo chown root foo`
- `ls -l foo`
- `cat foo`

You've just changed the user ownership to root, while keeping the group ownership. As the file has group- and world-read permissions, you can still see its contents.

Task 3:
Now run:

- `sudo chmod o-r foo`
- `ls -l foo`
- `cat foo`

That `chmod` command removes read permissions from foo. However, as you still have group ownership, you can still see the file's contents.

Task 4:
Now run:

- `sudo chgrp root foo`
- `sudo chmod 600 foo`
- `ls -l foo`
- `cat foo`

This `chmod` command sets the permissions explicitly, to read-write for the owning user only. As that is root, we can no longer read the file.

Task 5:
The default permissions for a newly created file can be adjusted with `umask`. This serves to "mask out," at a bit level, permissions that a new file should not have. Run the following

- `u=$(umask)`
- `umask 0777`
- `touch bar`
- `ls -l bar`
- `umask $u`

The bar file should have no permissions set—you've masked them all out with `umask`.

Task 6:
Finally, clean up with `sudo rm foo bar`

Notes:
The first octal bit of `chmod` deals with setuid and setgid (and the sticky bit, on directories). When set, these bits will run an executable file as the user/group owner, rather than the user running the executable. This opens up security risks, particularly when a program is owned by root. For this reason, most systems will ignore the setuid/setgid bits when set on shell scripts.

LAB 51

Directory Permissions

Lab Objective:
Learn how to manipulate permissions and ownership settings of directories.

Lab Purpose:
In this lab, you will learn to use `chmod`, `chown`, and `chgrp`, as well as `umask`, and their implications for directories.

Lab Tool:
Ubuntu 18.04 (or another distro of your choice)

Lab Topology:
A single Linux machine, or virtual machine

Lab Walkthrough:

Task 1:
Open the Terminal and run:

- `mkdir foo`
- `echo "Hello World" > foo/bar`
- `ls -la foo`

Look at the first field; you should see `drwxr-xr-x`

This indicates the user, group, and other permissions. The first 'd' just indicates a directory. The last nine characters, in groups of three, denote these permissions. In this instance:

- `rwx` indicates read/write/execute permissions for the user who owns the file
- `r-x` indicates read/execute permissions for the group that owns the file
- `r-x` indicates read/execute permissions for all non-owners, a.k.a. "world"

Who are the user and group owners of this file? The third and fourth fields of `ls -l` tell us that. By default, it should be your own user and primary group.

Task 2:
Now run:

- `sudo chown root foo`
- `ls -la foo`
- `cat foo/bar`

You've just changed the user ownership to root, while keeping the group ownership. As the directory has group- and world-read permissions, you can still see its contents.

Task 3:
Now run:

- `sudo chmod o-r foo`
- `ls -la foo`
- `cat foo/bar`

That `chmod` command removes read permissions from foo. However, as you still have group ownership, you can still see the file's contents.

Task 4:
Now run:

- `sudo chgrp root foo`
- `ls -la foo`
- `ls -ld foo`
- `cat foo/bar`

You've now set yourself up with execute-only permissions on the foo directory, which is an interesting scenario. You no longer have permissions to view the contents of the directory, nor to add new files to it... but if you already know that a given file exists, your permissions for that file still allow you to act on it. In this example, you can view the contents of foo/bar, and even still modify them! This also applies to any subdirectories under foo.

Task 5:
Now run:

- `sudo chmod 2777 foo`
- `touch foo/baz`
- `ls -l foo/baz`

What you did was set the setgid bit for this directory, which causes files created under it to have the same group ownership as the directory itself. In practice, this is a way to ensure a group of users sharing files doesn't have to worry as much about permissions.

Task 6:
The default permissions for a newly created file can be adjusted with `umask`. This serves to "mask out," at a bit level, permissions that a new file should not have. Run the following

- `u=$(umask)`
- `umask 0777`
- `mkdir bar`
- `ls -ld bar`
- `umask $u`

The bar directory should have no permissions set—you've masked them all out with `umask`.

Task 6:
Finally, clean up with `sudo rm -r foo bar`

Notes:
Another special bit specific to directories is called the sticky bit, which is covered in Lab 25. This bit, set on a world-writable directory, ensures that users can only remove or modify files that they themselves own. This is most useful on /tmp.

LAB 52

User Auditing

Lab Objective:
Learn how to manage and audit users and user restrictions.

Lab Purpose:
In this lab, you will review a variety of tools used to manage users and maintain security through limitations on their privileges.

Lab Tool:
Ubuntu 18.04 (or another distro of your choice)

Lab Topology:
A single Linux machine, or virtual machine

Lab Walkthrough:

Task 1:
Throughout most of these labs, you've used `sudo` to grant yourself root privileges for certain tasks. Now, it's finally time to learn how to configure it:

- `sudo useradd luser`
- `sudo visudo`
- Under the "User privilege specification", add the following line:
  `luser          ALL=NOPASSWD:/usr/sbin/useradd`
- `sudo su luser`
- `sudo useradd luser2`
- `exit`

In this sequence, you edited the /etc/sudoers configuration file safely with `visudo` (which you should always do—a syntax error in the sudoers file can lock you out of your own system!) The addition means that the 'luser' user can run `useradd` as root, without being prompted for a password. "ALL" here means that it can be run on "ALL" systems, which in this case is only one, since you aren't connected to a NIS domain.

After switching to luser, you should have been able to add another user seamlessly, without being prompted. If you tried any other `sudo` command, you would be prompted for a password and the command would fail altogether.

Task 2:
Now run (the first command should all be on one line):

- `sudo sh -c 'echo "luser hard nproc 2" >> /etc/security/limits.conf'`
- `sudo su luser`
- `ulimit -a`
- `sleep 10000 &`
- `sleep 10000 &`
- `exit`

Attempting to run the second `sleep`, you should have been greeted with a mysterious error about "Cannot fork". What's going on here? Your first command applied a limit of 2 user processes to the 'luser' user. The shell counts as one process, which means luser can't do a whole lot after that! This is why the first `sleep` was successful while the second one failed.

Remove the process limit from luser in /etc/security/limits.conf before moving on.

Task 3:
Now, a few commands to audit user activity and logins:

- `who -a`
- `w`
- `lastlog`

Task 4:
Finally, clean up:

- Run `sudo visudo` and delete the 'luser' line that you added
- `sudo userdel luser`
- `sudo userdel luser2`

Notes:
If you are unable to delete user "luser" at the end of the lab, because the user is still used by a process, you can find the PID being called to kill. luser needs to log out before deletion.

LAB 53

SSH

Lab Objective:
Learn how to operate OpenSSH to create a secure network tunnel.

Lab Purpose:
In this lab, you will learn about OpenSSH, a common tool for creating secure connections and tunnels to/from Linux servers.

Lab Tool:
Ubuntu 18.04 (or another distro of your choice)

Lab Topology:
A single Linux machine, or virtual machine

Lab Walkthrough:

Task 1:
First, install openssh-server: `sudo apt install openssh-server`

Now run: `ssh-keygen -t ed25519`

You can save your user's SSH key in the default location, but make sure to choose a password—you will use this later.

Copy the public key into authorized_keys to allow yourself SSH access: `cp .ssh/id_ed25519.pub .ssh/authorized_keys`

Finally, get your machine's host keys:

```
ssh-keyscan localhost | ssh-keygen -lf -
```

Save the bottom three lines somewhere; those are your host key fingerprints, in different formats, and you will use one of them later.

Task 2:
Now run:

- `eval $(ssh-agent)`
- `ssh-add`
- Type your password. This will cache your SSH private key to `ssh-agent` so you don't have to type the password again during this session (while maintaining its security).

Finally, connect with SSH: `ssh localhost`

You should be prompted to confirm a previously unknown host key. Compare this key with the three host keys you saved from Task 1; one of them should be a match. (If not, something has gone wrong.) Assuming so, confirm the connection and you should now be connected locally over SSH, without having to type your password again.

Task 3:
Run `exit`, then run `ssh localhost` again just to be sure you can connect with no prompts. Now run:

- `exit`
- `kill $SSH_AGENT_PID`
- `ssh localhost`

Did you have to type your password this time to unlock your key?

Notes:
Make sure you can follow and understand all the steps that are happening in this fairly complex process:

- Installing the OpenSSH server. This step generates host keys automatically.
- Generating a keypair for your user, and granting yourself access by creating an authorized_keys file containing the public key.
- Getting the server's host key fingerprints for later verification.
- Initializing the `ssh-agent` caching tool and adding your private key to it.
- Connecting over SSH (even if to localhost), verifying the host key, and permanently saving the fingerprint.

LAB 54

GPG

Lab Objective:
Learn how to operate GPG for data encryption and verification.

Lab Purpose:
In this lab, you will learn about GnuPG, a tool used to encrypt, decrypt, sign, and verify data of files, e-mails, and package updates, among other things.

Lab Tool:
Ubuntu 18.04 (or another distro of your choice)

Lab Topology:
A single Linux machine, or virtual machine

Lab Walkthrough:

Task 1:
Open the Terminal and run: `gpg --generate-key`

You will be prompted for a name and e-mail address, then GPG will do the rest. Afterwards, run `gpg --generate-key` again to create a second key for a different fictitious person.

List the keys you created with `gpg -k`

Finally, take a peek at ~/.gnupg. In this directory, you should see a trust database (trustdb.gpg) and public keyring (pubring.kbx), as well as an openpgp-revocs.d directory for revocation certificates, and private-keys-v1.d directory containing your private key files.

Task 2:

Now let's try sending a secret message between your two imaginary GPG users:

- `echo "Hello World" > secret`
- `gpg -se -r [email2] secret`
- `file secret.gpg`
- `gpg -d < secret.gpg`

In this scenario, a file has been sent from [email1] to [email2]. You signed and then encrypted the file with the second user's public key; secret.gpg was the result, which, as `file` should tell you, is a PGP RSA encrypted session key. Finally, you decrypt this file and are shown an encryption header, and the message itself, followed by a signature (which GPG informs you is good).

Notes:

In a real-world scenario, you would be importing keys either from a third-party directly or from a public keyserver, and then assigning them trust values. "Trust" in GPG-speak means "How much do you trust this person to properly verify someone else's key before signing it?" Recommended research: the web of trust.

LAB 55

Pluggable Authentication Modules

Lab Objective:
Learn how to configure PAM and its modules.

Lab Purpose:
In this lab, you will explore Linux Pluggable Authentication Modules, their purpose, and configuration.

Lab Tool:
Ubuntu 18.04 (or another distro of your choice)

Lab Topology:
A single Linux machine, or virtual machine

Lab Walkthrough:

Task 1:
First, investigate a simple PAM configuration file, which should already be present on your system: `cat /etc/pam.d/common-password`

Now make a backup of this file. You'll use it later:

```
sudo cp /etc/pam.d/common-password{,.bak}
```

Task 2:
Install the PAM module for a library called Cracklib:

```
sudo apt install libpam-cracklib
```

Cracklib is a tool for enforcing strong password security. When you installed its PAM module, the package manager should have changed the relevant configuration files as well. Take a look at some of those changes:

```
diff /etc/pam.d/common-password*
```

You should see one new line...

```
password    requisite    pam_cracklib.so retry=3 minlen=8 difok=3
```

... and one changed line:

```
password    [success=1 default=ignore]    pam_unix.so obscure use_
authtok try_first_pass sha512
```

The new line for pam_cracklib.so has been placed first in this file (excluding comments), for good reason. You see the "requisite" flag? That means password changes that don't pass muster will immediately fail, and none of the modules after this line will be triggered. If a secure password is used, then PAM will continue testing the other modules according to its rules. That's exactly what you want to happen in this case.

What about the new "use_authtok" and "try_first_pass" options in the second line? Those ensure that pam_unix.so sets a user's password to the one that has already passed Cracklib, rather than prompting the user again.

Task 3:
Now run `passwd` and try to change your password to a simple dictionary word, like "password". What happens?

Task 4:
Clean up that extra backup file: `sudo rm /etc/pam.d/common-password.bak`

You can also remove the Cracklib module, if you don't want to keep it (it's not the worst thing to keep around): `sudo apt remove libpam-cracklib`

Notes:
On a modern Ubuntu system, you may manage some PAM config files using the `pam-auth-update` tool.

LAB 56

OpenVPN

Lab Objective:
Learn how to configure a popular VPN client called OpenVPN.

Lab Purpose:
In this lab, you will configure a Linux OpenVPN client connection. However, before you can do that, you need something for the client to connect to...

Lab Tool:
Ubuntu 18.04 (or another distro of your choice), and resources for a second VM to be set up during this lab.

Lab Topology:
Two Linux machines accessible via the same network.

Lab Walkthrough:

Task 1:
Before you can set up an OpenVPN client, you will first need a server for that client to connect to. Complex VPN server configuration is beyond the scope of this lab, but fortunately there's an easier way:

1. Download a pre-configured OpenVPN VM from TurnkeyLinux. You want the OVA file, which will work with VirtualBox: **https://www.turnkeylinux.org/download?file=turnkey-openvpn-15.1-stretch-amd64.ova**
2. Follow these instructions to create the VM in VirtualBox. You will be deploying a VM-optimized image: **https://www.turnkeylinux.org/docs/installation-appliances-virtualbox**
3. Launch the new VM and run through the setup process, following the on-screen prompts. Most prompts are self-explanatory, but be sure to select the "server" profile and type the server's IP address correctly. The subnets you choose don't really matter, as long as they don't overlap with your local network. You may skip the TurnkeyLinux API and the e-mail notifications.

4. Now you have an OpenVPN server running! You can quit the setup menu and log in via terminal, which you will use in the next task.

Task 2:
At the terminal prompt (as root) on your OpenVPN VM, run:

```
openvpn-addclient lab56 101labs@example.com
```

You've just created client information on the server, which also results in a configuration file containing all the information the client itself needs. Now, you just need to get that file to the client.

On the client VM, run:

- `sudo apt install openvpn`
- `sudo scp root@[serverIP]:/etc/openvpn/easy-rsa/keys/lab56.ovpn /etc/openvpn/lab56.conf`

Note that the previous command is all on one line. You will be prompted for the password to the OpenVPN VM, and then the file will be copied to its correct location.

IMPORTANT: If this step does not work, then you have configured the virtual network incorrectly, or there is a problem on your local network. By default, neither your lab VM nor the TurnkeyLinux VM should have any firewalls interfering with connectivity.

Task 3:
Now open and view the /etc/openvpn/lab56.conf file in your favorite editor. Make sure the first line contains the correct server IP, and change it if it does not.

The first few lines of this file should look something like this:

```
remote 192.168.10.1 1194
proto udp
remote-cert-tls server
client
dev tun
resolv-retry infinite
keepalive 10 120
nobind
```

```
comp-lzo
verb 3
```

After this are maybe a few other options plus your client's private key, public certificate, and the server certificate(s). These are required for the client and server to authenticate each other, but not particularly interesting from a configuration standpoint.

The key option here is that very first line, where you specify the remote server and port. In various situations, you might also need to change the `proto` or `dev` options (and of course the `client` and `nobind` options, if you are running a server). But, for the most part, this client configuration is pretty standard.

Task 4:
Finally, to start OpenVPN, run:

```
sudo openvpn /etc/openvpn/lab56.conf
```

You will see a lot of output, but if all went well, the final line should include "Initialization Sequence Completed."

Open up another tab or terminal window to test your connection. First, run:

```
ip addr show
```

In this list, you should see a new tunnel device. The name will vary, but typically it starts with "tun". On Ubuntu, it should be called "tun0". This tun0 device should have an IP address assigned to it by the OpenVPN server, via DHCP. Take this IP and swap out the last number for a 1—typically, this is the OpenVPN server's private network IP. (But not always. To confirm this, run `ip addr show` on the server itself.) In any case, this is *not* the same IP that is in your client configuration. The server and client are using their own new addresses as part of this **V**irtual **P**rivate **N**etwork.

Once you've determined the server's private IP, try connecting to it:

- `ping [serverIP]`
- `ssh root@[serverIP]`

If you can connect to the OpenVPN server, via its VPN address, in these ways, then you know your VPN is working.

Task 5:

To close out, hit Ctrl+C on your client's OpenVPN process to kill it. You can then of course remove the /etc/openvpn/lab56.conf file, uninstall OpenVPN, and shut down the server as well.

Notes:

Another common VPN protocol is IPsec. IPsec is arguably more difficult to learn and set up, but worth the effort. It is left as an exercise to the reader to find (or create!) a "turnkey" IPsec server to test.

LAB 57

Best Practices (SSH)

Lab Objective:
Learn about best practices for an SSH server and how to adhere to them.

Lab Purpose:
In this lab, you will use a tool called Lynis to scan for and resolve potential security weaknesses in your SSH configuration.

Lab Tool:
Ubuntu 18.04 (or another distro of your choice)

Lab Topology:
A single Linux machine, or virtual machine

Lab Walkthrough:

Task 1:
First, install the Lynis security scanning tool: `sudo apt install lynis`

Now, use it to scan for potential SSH security problems (all on one line):

```
sudo lynis audit system --tests-from-category security --tests-from-
group ssh
```

There's a lot of output here, but what's under the "Warnings" and "Suggestions" headings is what you're interested in. There are several suggestions, and the SSH scan is particularly nice because it describes exactly how to modify your configuration to solve the problem! This lab will focus on these changes:

- AllowTcpForwarding (YES --> NO)
- ClientAliveCountMax (3 --> 2)
- Compression (YES --> (DELAYED|NO))
- LogLevel (INFO --> VERBOSE)

- MaxAuthTries (6 --> 2)
- MaxSessions (10 --> 2)
- PermitRootLogin (WITHOUT-PASSWORD --> NO)
- Port (22 -->)
- TCPKeepAlive (YES --> NO)
- X11Forwarding (YES --> NO)
- AllowAgentForwarding (YES --> NO)

Task 2:
To make the changes, open the /etc/ssh/sshd_config file, as root, in your favorite editor. Change each of the following lines, as described:

- #AllowTcpForwarding yes
  AllowTcpForwarding no

- #AllowAgentForwarding yes
  AllowAgentForwarding no

- #ClientAliveCountMax 3
  ClientAliveCountMax 2

- #Compression delayed
  Compression no

- #LogLevel INFO
  LogLevel VERBOSE

- #MaxAuthTries 6
  MaxAuthTries 2

- #MaxSessions 10
  MaxSessions 2

- #PermitRootLogin prohibit-password
  PermitRootLogin no

- #Port 22
  Port 2222

- #TCPKeepAlive yes
  TCPKeepAlive no

- X11Forwarding yes
  X11Forwarding no

Save the file, quit the editor, and codify your changes with:

```
sudo systemctl reload sshd
```

Task 3:
Now run that scan again:

```
sudo lynis audit system --tests-from-category security --tests-from-
group ssh
```

Did you get a perfect score? Great! Now you're done... right?

Well, maybe. But if you were to implement these changes on a real-world server, you should probably take note of what you just did (ideally before you do it), right? For example, you've just changed SSH's listening port to 2222, and disabled root logins and X11 over SSH. Better let your coworkers know!

Notes:
Your scan results may show more or fewer warnings/suggestions than what's listed here. Please feel free to implement any and all suggestions on your own lab machine.

LAB 58

Best Practices (Authentication)

Lab Objective:
Learn about best practices for user authentication and how to adhere to them.

Lab Purpose:
In this lab, you will use a tool called Lynis to scan for and resolve potential security weaknesses in your user authentication configuration.

Lab Tool:
Ubuntu 18.04 (or another distro of your choice)

Lab Topology:
A single Linux machine, or virtual machine

Lab Walkthrough:

Task 1:
First, install the Lynis security scanning tool: `sudo apt install lynis`

Now, use it to scan for potential user authentication security problems (all on one line):

```
sudo lynis audit system --tests-from-category security --tests-from-
group authentication
```

There's a lot of output here, but what's under the "Warnings" and "Suggestions" headings is what you're interested in. There are several suggestions, but this lab will focus on the following changes:

- Install a PAM module for password strength testing like pam_cracklib or pam_passwdqc
- Configure minimum password age in /etc/login.defs
- Configure maximum password age in /etc/login.defs
- Default umask in /etc/login.defs could be more strict like 027

Task 2:
Start with the low-hanging fruit by installing pam_cracklib:

```
sudo apt install libpam-cracklib
```

One down, three to go!

Now, open /etc/login.defs in your favorite editor (as root) and change the min/max password age. Change the `PASS_MAX_DAYS` line to `90`, and the `PASS_MIN_DAYS` line to `1`. While you're here, change the `UMASK` line to `027` as well, to knock out the last suggestion.

Task 3:
Now run that scan again:

```
sudo lynis audit system --tests-from-category security --tests-from-
group authentication
```

Did you get a perfect score? Great! Now you're done... right?

Well, maybe. But if you were to implement these changes on a real-world server, you should probably take note of what you just did (ideally before you do it), right? For example, you've just forced all the users of this machine to change their passwords every 90 days. Better let your coworkers know!

Notes:
Your scan results may show more or fewer warnings/suggestions than what's listed here. Please feel free to implement any and all suggestions on your own lab machine.

LAB 59

Best Practices (Auditing)

Lab Objective:
Learn about best practices for system auditing and how to adhere to them.

Lab Purpose:
In this lab, you will use a tool called Lynis to scan for and resolve issues in your auditing configuration.

Lab Tool:
Ubuntu 18.04 (or another distro of your choice)

Lab Topology:
A single Linux machine, or virtual machine

Lab Walkthrough:

Task 1:
First, install the Lynis security scanning tool: `sudo apt install lynis`

Now, use it to scan for potential system accounting problems (all on one line):

```
sudo lynis audit system --tests-from-category security --tests-from-
group accounting
```

There's a lot of output here, but what's under the "Warnings" and "Suggestions" headings is what you're interested in. There are several suggestions, but this lab will focus on the following changes:

- Enable process accounting
- Enable sysstat to collect accounting (no results)
- Enable auditd to collect audit information

Task 2:
Resolving these issues is as simple as installing a few packages to enhance the system's accounting/audit capabilities:

```
sudo apt install acct sysstat auditd
```

To enable sysstat, open the /etc/default/sysstat file in your favorite editor and just change `ENABLED="false"` to `ENABLED="true"`.

Now run that scan again:

```
sudo lynis audit system --tests-from-category security --tests-from-group accounting
```

You may discover, in both labs and in the real world, that sometimes solving one problem only unearths a different problem... and that is exactly the case here. Lynis should now complain about another issue:

- Audit daemon is enabled with an empty ruleset. Disable the daemon or define rules

Naturally, an auditing system is meant to be used and analyzed, not just sit there sending data to /dev/null. To resolve these last two issues, you'll need to configure it.

A full configuration of auditd is outside the scope of this lab; there are plenty of good rulesets online, and some packages come with their own. For now, just edit the /etc/audit/rules.d/audit.rules file and add a simple line to the end to audit the audit logs:

```
-w /var/log/audit -k auditlog
```

Now restart auditd to regenerate its own audit.rules file:

```
sudo systemctl restart auditd
```

Task 3:
Finally, run that Lynis scan one more time:

```
sudo lynis audit system --tests-from-category security --tests-from-group accounting
```

Notes:
Your scan results may show more or fewer warnings/suggestions than what's listed here. Please feel free to implement any and all suggestions on your own lab machine.

LAB 60

System Messaging and Logging

Lab Objective:
Learn how to view system messages and logs.

Lab Purpose:
In this lab, you will learn how to debug your system (or just get a glimpse at what's going on) by viewing log messages.

Lab Tool:
Ubuntu 18.04 (or another distro of your choice)

Lab Topology:
A single Linux machine, or virtual machine

Lab Walkthrough:

Task 1:
Open your Terminal and run `dmesg`

The `man` (manual) page for `dmesg` states that it is used to "examine or control the kernel ring buffer." To put it simply, you can use `dmesg` to view boot logs and other logs your distro considers important.

Task 2:
Run `ls -aR /var/log`

This is the main storage directory for all system logs (although, see the Notes). If you peruse some of the log files, you may find some of the same logs that were printed by `dmesg`. In particular, look at the `/var/log/syslog` file.

Configuration of `rsyslog` is outside the scope of this lab, but through `rsyslog` you can record logs of all severities, write them to different files, e-mail them, or even print emergency alert messages to the console for all users to see.

Task 3:
You can use `tail` to monitor logs in real-time. Run: `sudo tail -f /var/log/auth.log`

Then, in a separate Terminal window or tab, run `sudo -i` three times. When prompted for your password, do each of the following once:

- Type Ctrl+C to cancel the command.
- Intentionally mistype your password.
- Type your password correctly.

Check the tab where `tail` is running to see what is logged as a result of your actions. This is a simple, but accurate, method of keeping tabs on `sudo` users on a system.

Notes:
In recent years, traditional logging tools have been supplanted in some distros by `systemd`, which uses `journalctl` to manage logs. In practice, you should familiarize yourself with both log management techniques.

LAB 61

Rsyslog

Lab Objective:
Learn how to configure the `rsyslog` logging daemon.

Lab Purpose:
In this lab, you will learn about basic configuration of `rsyslog` and its different logging options.

Lab Tool:
Ubuntu 18.04 (or another distro of your choice)

Lab Topology:
A single Linux machine, or virtual machine

Lab Walkthrough:

Task 1:
Open two Terminal windows/tabs.

In the first one, run: `tail -f /var/log/syslog`

In the second one, run: `logger "Hello World"`

Now go back to the first tab. Did your friendly message show up in the system logs? Hit Ctrl+C to exit `tail`.

`logger` is a generic utility for sending logs to a number of daemons, including `rsyslog`, and `journald`, which we will discuss in Lab 63.

Task 2:
Now look at the configuration:

```
grep -v -e ^# -e ^$ /etc/rsyslog.conf /etc/rsyslog.d/*
```

This may vary by distro—once you locate the correct file(s), you may want to open them with a text editor.

Ultimately, you are looking for a file such as 50-default.conf or similar, defining what facilities log to what files. On Ubuntu, this file should contain a line like:

```
auth,authpriv.*                 /var/log/auth.log
```

At the top of this file, add the following line:

```
*.*                             /var/log/allthelogs
```

Then restart the daemon: `systemctl restart rsyslog`

Wait a few minutes (or create your own logs with `logger`), then check the contents of /var/log/allthelogs. This should be an amalgamation of all the logs which are going to many other log files.

Task 3:
Clean up by deleting the line you added to the `rsyslog` config, and run `systemctl restart rsyslog`

Notes:
Aside from `journald`, which most distros have migrated to as a result of Systemd, there are also other logging daemons like `syslog` and `syslog-ng`. While some daemons have their own configuration formats, all at least support the classic syslog configuration format (and that should be what you saw in `rsyslog`'s own configs). Learn that format, and you will have learned configuration for all of the major logging daemons.

LAB 62

Logrotate

Lab Objective:
Learn how to configure the `logrotate` to rotate system logs.

Lab Purpose:
`logrotate` is a commonly used tool to rotate logs, i.e. archive them every X days/weeks and delete them every Y weeks/months. In this lab, you will learn how to configure it.

Lab Tool:
Ubuntu 18.04 (or another distro of your choice)

Lab Topology:
A single Linux machine, or virtual machine

Lab Walkthrough:

Task 1:
Open the Terminal and run `cat /etc/logrotate.conf`

This is the main logrotate configuration file, the one that contains the default directives. You may see lines like:

```
weekly
rotate 4
create
```

In combination, these lines will save an archive of some log file every week, keep each archive for four weeks, and create a new empty log file after rotating an older one.

Additionally, you probably have a directory called /etc/logrotate.d, where some package-specific configs are stored. Ubuntu has one for `apt`, so look at /etc/logrotate.d/apt, or another file of your choosing.

You might see directives here like `rotate 12` (keep for 12 weeks instead of 4, or 12 months if it includes `monthly`), `compress` to compress the archives, or `notifempty` to ignore the log if it is empty.

See `man logrotate` for more details.

Task 2:
Now, with `sudo` (or `sudoedit`), open a text editor and create a file called /etc/logrotate.d/mylog with the following contents:

```
/var/log/mylog.log {
  hourly
  su root syslog
  rotate 2
  create
  compress
  missingok
}
```

Then: `sudo touch /var/log/mylog.log`

Normally you'd have to wait at least an hour to see any rotation happen, but you can force the situation with the `-f` switch. Run:

- `sudo logrotate -fv /etc/logrotate.d/mylog`
- `ls -al /var/log/mylog*`

You should see a compressed archive of the original file, as mylog.log.1.gz, and a new log called mylog.log. Run that first command twice more. The second time you run it will create a second archive file, but on the third run you should see a line at the bottom saying "removing old log /var/log/mylog.log.3.gz", as per the configuration file.

Task 3:
Finally, clean up: `sudo rm /etc/logrotate.d/mylog /var/log/mylog*`

Notes:
Typically, `logrotate` is run via a daily cron job. Can you find where this cron job is configured on your system? (Hint: See Lab 40!)

LAB 63

Journald

Lab Objective:
Learn how to manage and read data from `journald`, the Systemd logger.

Lab Purpose:
In this lab, you will get to know `journald`, the Systemd logging system that is slowly replacing classic `syslog` variants in most Linux distros.

Lab Tool:
Ubuntu 18.04 (or another distro of your choice)

Lab Topology:
A single Linux machine, or virtual machine

Lab Walkthrough:

Task 1:
Open two Terminal windows/tabs.

In the first one, run: `journalctl -f`

In the second one, run: `systemd-cat echo "Hello World"`

Now go back to the first tab. Did your friendly message show up in the system logs? Hit Ctrl+C to exit.

`systemd-cat` is a convenient tool, like `logger`, that can send output directly to the `journald` logs.

Task 2:
Now look at the configuration: `cat /etc/systemd/journald.conf`

On a default Ubuntu 18.04 system, you will probably see... a lot of commented-out lines. This is just the default configuration, which can still tell you a lot. You can learn the meaning of these options from `man journald.conf`, which is conveniently laid out in the same order as the config file.

Use the two tabs from Task 1, or open a second tab if necessary. In the first tab, run `tty`, then save the value it prints out for later.

In the second tab, open /etc/systemd/journald.conf for editing as root (via `sudo` or `sudoedit`). Append these two lines to the bottom of the file:

```
ForwardToConsole=yes
TTYPath=[tty]
```

... where `[tty]` is the value printed by `tty` in the other tab. Save and quit the editor, then run:

- `sudo systemctl restart systemd-journald`
- `systemd-cat echo "Hello World"`

Now look back at the first tab again. You should see logs being printed directly to your console! This can be useful for monitoring system logs, generally, without having to keep a process running.

Task 3:
Clean up:

- Edit /etc/systemd/journald.conf again and delete the two lines you added
- Run `sudo systemctl restart systemd-journald`

Notes:
When stored persistently on the disk (which is typically what you want to do, as opposed to only storing logs in memory), `journald` logs are stored in /var/log/journal. If you try to read these files, however, you will quickly notice that they are not the text logs you may be used to! Somewhat inconveniently, `journald` stores its logs in a binary format which is only readable by systemd-related tools.

LAB 64

Ports and Services

Lab Objective:
Learn how to gather information on ports and services on a Linux system.

Lab Purpose:
In this lab, you will examine some common networking principles, namely ports and services, using some Linux command-line tools.

Lab Tool:
Ubuntu 18.04 (or another distro of your choice)

Lab Topology:
A single Linux machine, or virtual machine

Lab Walkthrough:

Task 1:
Open the terminal and run: `sudo ss -Saputn`

This is a list of currently open connections and listening ports on your machine. There's a lot of output here, but you're mostly interested in the first column and the last three columns.

The first column lists what protocol each connection follows. Most likely this will be either UDP or TCP, which you may recall are faster/connectionless and more-reliable/connection-oriented, respectively.

Columns 5 and 6 list your IP:port and the remote host's IP:port. TCP and UDP each have 65,535 ports available, some of which are assigned (either officially, by IANA, or unofficially by common use) to various services.

Look at the port numbers and try to identify which services are using each "server" port. The server port is important, because the client port (the port from which a client first makes a connection) is usually dynamic. It may help to look at column 7 to see what process on your machine is using the connection.

Task 2:
Programs commonly use the /etc/services file to map service names to the port(s) they should listen or connect on. The file is human-readable, however, so you should look yourself.

By looking through /etc/services (with `cat /etc/services`), can you identify what services your machine was listening for, or connecting to, in Task 1? Can you identify which ports are used by common services, such as HTTP, SSH, LDAP, SNMP, and SMTP?

Task 3:
Another very common protocol is one that you won't find any listening ports for... because it doesn't have ports! This is ICMP, a.k.a. "ping" (though in reality, it is used for much more than pinging).

Open two terminal windows/tabs. In the first one, run: `sudo tcpdump -n -i any icmp`

In the second one, run: `ping -c 5 localhost`

Go back to the first tab, and you should see the requests and replies from your pings—and maybe some other ICMP traffic too, if you're lucky.

Notes:
If you couldn't see any traffic or get any ICMP replies in the last task, a firewall on your machine may be to blame. Blocking ICMP traffic indiscriminately like that is a poor practice, so it's an exercise to the student to figure out how to open that up a little. (Hint: `iptables`)

LAB 65

iptables

Lab Objective:
Learn how to configure and view rules for iptables, the standard Linux firewall.

Lab Purpose:
In this lab, you will explore how to view, add, remove, and modify iptables firewall rules.

Lab Tool:
Ubuntu 18.04 (or another distro of your choice)

Lab Topology:
A single Linux machine, or virtual machine

Lab Walkthrough:

Task 1:
Open the Terminal and run: `sudo iptables -nL`

The output you receive should look something like this:

```
Chain INPUT (policy ACCEPT)
target     prot opt source               destination

Chain FORWARD (policy ACCEPT)
target     prot opt source               destination

Chain OUTPUT (policy ACCEPT)
target     prot opt source               destination
```

IMPORTANT: If you see any firewall rules or policies other than the default ACCEPT as shown above (filter table only), you will need to start with a "clean slate." Run the following commands to reset the filter table to a default state:

- `sudo iptables -F`
- `sudo iptables -X`
- `sudo iptables -P INPUT ACCEPT`
- `sudo iptables -P FORWARD ACCEPT`
- `sudo iptables -P OUTPUT ACCEPT`

Note that, if any rules were changed here, you can typically get back your system's firewall rules by restarting the `iptables` or `firewalld` service. On a default Ubuntu 18.04 system, this should not be necessary.

Task 2:
Now you will experiment with firewall rules on ICMP (also known, somewhat incorrectly, as "ping"). First, make sure you can ping your local system:

```
ping -c 1 127.0.0.1
```

You should quickly get a response indicating your ping was successful. Now add a firewall rule to the filter table's INPUT chain to drop all ICMP, as follows:

```
sudo iptables -A INPUT -p icmp -j DROP
```

And try that ping command again: `ping -c 1 127.0.0.1`

This time, you will have to wait several seconds for any output, and that output should indicate that no response was received. As you might expect, your local firewall simply dropped the ICMP request it received, never sending a reply. However, that isn't the only way that a firewall can block traffic...

- `sudo iptables -R INPUT 1 -p icmp --icmp-type echo-request -j REJECT`
- `ping -c 1 127.0.0.1`

This time, you should receive a response indicating "Destination Port Unreachable." As per the name, your machine has explicitly rejected the ping. (Special exercise: Can you figure out why the "`--icmp-type echo-request`" flag is required here?)

Finally, delete this rule with: `sudo iptables -D INPUT 1`

Task 3:
It is quite common to add rules to the INPUT table, but less common to do so on the OUTPUT table. However, doing so is a good security practice. Add a REJECT rule here as before: `sudo iptables -A OUTPUT -p icmp -j REJECT`

And test:

- `ping -c 1 127.0.0.1`
- `ping -c 1 101labs.net`

Another exercise: Does adding "`--icmp-type echo-request`" here, as in Task 2, change the responses? Why or why not?

Finally, delete this rule as well with: `sudo iptables -D OUTPUT 1`

Notes:
`iptables` is a powerful tool with many additional options and modules. In practice, on a secure system, you would set default DROP policies (e.g. `iptables -P INPUT DROP`) and whitelist traffic as appropriate, adding additional chains if the complexity warranted it. The nat table is also well worth exploring.

LAB 66

UFW

Lab Objective:
Learn how to manage `ufw`, a more user-friendly way to configure iptables.

Lab Purpose:
In this lab, you will practice using UFW (Uncomplicated Firewall) as an alternative way of managing Linux firewall rules.

Lab Tool:
Ubuntu 18.04 (or another distro of your choice)

Lab Topology:
A single Linux machine, or virtual machine

Lab Walkthrough:

Task 1:
First, make sure UFW is enabled (by default, it is not): `sudo ufw enable`

You can confirm the status with: `sudo ufw status verbose`

Now take a peek at the actual firewall rules UFW has set up: `sudo iptables -nL`

If you did Lab 65, you have a pretty good idea of the (sparse) rulesets that your OS had set up by default. Enabling UFW alone made a lot of changes! The rules themselves aren't terribly complex, but the way they are presented can make them difficult for a human to analyze directly. You can see this output, slightly modified, with `sudo ufw show raw`

Task 2:
The syntax for adding rules via UFW is rather simple:

- `sudo ufw deny 12345`
- `sudo ufw status`
- `sudo iptables -nL | grep 12345`

It's not obvious from the last command, but UFW has added two DROP rules (one for TCP, one for UDP) to the `ufw-user-input` chain.

You can also add rules for applications based on profiles, even accounting for those applications changing their listening ports (or you not remembering what those ports are):

- `sudo ufw app info OpenSSH`
- `sudo ufw allow OpenSSH`
- `sudo ufw status`
- `sudo iptables -nL | grep OpenSSH`

Task 3:
Finally, clean up the extra rules you added with: `sudo ufw reset`

If you don't wish to keep UFW, disable it with: `sudo ufw disable`

This will clear UFW's rules, but not its chains. To do that, run:

- `sudo iptables -F`
- `sudo iptables -X`

Note that UFW only ever operates on the filter table, so you don't need to worry about any other rules/chains polluting the other tables.

Notes:
You can change some of UFW's options, including default policies and whether it manages the built-in chains (INPUT, OUTPUT, FORWARD) in `/etc/default/ufw`. The application profiles, should you need to change their ports, are stored in `/etc/ufw/applications.d/`

LAB 67

Archiving and Unarchiving

Lab Objective:
Learn how to create, extract, and examine various types of archive files.

Lab Purpose:
In this lab, you will learn about gzip, bzip2, and xz compressed archives—as well as two tools, `tar` and `cpio`, to manage most Linux archive types.

Lab Tool:
Ubuntu 18.04 (or another distro of your choice)

Lab Topology:
A single Linux machine, or virtual machine

Lab Walkthrough:

Task 1:
Open the Terminal application and run the following:

```
mkdir lab45
cd lab45
touch f1 f2 f3 f4 f5 f6 f7 f8 f9
```

Task 2:
Though ZIP is a common format and well-supported on Linux, it is not the main compression format Linux uses. That would be the classic gzip:

```
gzip f*
ls
```

Wait a minute... why are there now nine gzipped files instead of just one? And what happened to the originals?

This is why gzip is considered a *compression* format rather than an *archive* one. To create a single, easy-to-use archive file, we need a different tool...

Task 3:
Run: `tar -cf files.tar.gz f*`

Now, with the help of the *tar archiver*, you have your gzipped archive in files.tar.gz... well, sort of.

Normally, with a gzipped tarball, you would be able to extract it with `tar -xf files.tar.gz` and get all of the original files back. Instead, you could try that yourself now, and you would get the nine .gz files.

There's a better way. Let's blow this up and start over:

```
rm f*
touch f1 f2 f3 f4 f5 f6 f7 f8 f9
tar -czf archive.tar.gz f*
tar --list -f archive.tar.gz
```

Ta-da! Now you see a list of nine files within your single compressed tarball.

Task 4:
gzip isn't the only format you can use with `tar`:

```
tar -cjf archive.tar.bz2 f*
tar -cJf archive.tar.xz f*
```

The bzip2 and XZ formats, respectively, are newer and use different algorithms from gzip, but the end result is the same. `tar` can extract all of its formats in the same way, simply by using `tar -xf filename`.

Task 5:
`cpio` is another archiving tool used, most notably, in the RPM package manager and `initramfs`. Run:

- `find . | cpio -o > lab45.cpio`
- `cpio -t < lab45.cpio`
- `rm f1`
- `cpio -i -d f1 < lab45.cpio`

- `rm f*`
- `cpio -i -vd < lab45.cpio`

In short, what you are doing here is creating an archive, listing that archive (with `-t`), extracting the f1 file, and then extracting all of the files.

Task 6:
Another useful command for backups is `dd`. Typically this is used for block-level copying of an entire disk or partition, but it can also be used with ordinary files:

```
dd if=f1 of=f1.bak
```

Of course, if that's all you were doing, you could just use `cp`. A more typical usage would be something like (**do not actually run this**):

```
dd if=/dev/sda1 of=/dev/sdb1
```

Assuming you had already connected a backup drive, this would copy the entire /dev/sda1 partition onto it.

Task 7:
Finally, clean up:

```
cd ~
rm -r lab45
```

Notes:
To use compression-only without `tar` for archiving, each format has its own compression and decompression commands. Use `gzip/gunzip`, `bzip2/bunzip2`, and `xz/unxz`, for gzip, bzip2, and LZMA formats, respectively.

LAB 68

Remote Backups

Lab Objective:
Learn how to copy files and directories to a remote system for secure backups.

Lab Purpose:
In this lab, you will practice using three tools (`sftp`, `scp`, and `rsync`) to copy backups to a remote system.

Lab Tool:
Ubuntu 18.04 (or another distro of your choice)

Lab Topology:
A single Linux machine, or virtual machine

Lab Walkthrough:

Task 1:
First, set up the lab data:

- `mkdir -p lab68/bar`
- `echo hello > lab68/foo`
- `echo goodbye > lab68/bar/baz`

Task 2:
Now practice using SFTP to copy this new directory to a "remote" system:

- `sftp localhost`
- At the interactive prompt: `put -r lab68 lab68.bak`
- `quit`

Verify that the backup is present: `ls -l lab68.bak`

Finally, remove it, so it can be created in the next task: `rm -r lab68.bak`

Task 3:
With SFTP, you had to use an interactive prompt to push the files. This can be annoying for automation, and is also limited in terms of features. Fortunately, there's a better way:

```
scp -pr lab68 localhost:~/lab68.bak
```

Using SCP, you can accomplish the same task in a single command. This also adds the `-p` switch (also supported by SFTP) to preserve permissions and access times, which is useful for backups.

Next, you'll use what is arguably the most popular Linux backup tool, for good reason! Remove the backup directory once again: `rm -r lab68.bak`

Task 4:
Give `rsync` a go with: `rsync -av lab68/ localhost:~/lab68.bak`

Verify with: `ls -l lab68.bak`

Did you forget to put the / after `lab68`? If so, the results may not be what you expect! If you do that, `rsync` copies the directory path itself, not just the contents. This can be useful if you don't need to change the name, e.g.:

- `rsync -av lab68 localhost:~/tmp`
- `ls -l /tmp/lab68`

But perhaps the most unique feature of `rsync` is its synchronization ability. Observe:

- `echo "Hello World" > lab68/foo`
- `rsync -av lab68/ localhost:~/lab68.bak`

What do you notice about the output, compared to your first run? `rsync` begins by calculating a list of what files have changed. In this case, the incremental file list shows only `foo`, and this is the only file transferred! SFTP and SCP will happily overwrite your old backups if you tell them to do so, whether anything has changed or not. `rsync` is more efficient, and thus very useful for large backups. If you run this same command a third time, nothing (except access metadata) will be copied at all.

Finally, clean up: `rm -rf lab68*`

Notes:

`rsync` has a large number of options that are well worth getting to know. In particular, you may want to understand what metadata can be preserved (or not), how files vs. directories are managed, and the difference between copying, synchronizing, and mirroring.

Linux Troubleshooting and Diagnostics

LAB 69

Network Monitoring

Lab Objective:

Learn how to monitor network traffic on a Linux system.

Lab Purpose:

In this lab, you will experiment with `tcpdump`, a tool for sniffing and dumping network traffic metadata.

Lab Tool:

Ubuntu 18.04 (or another distro of your choice)

Lab Topology:

A single Linux machine, or virtual machine

Lab Walkthrough:

Task 1:

You may need to install `tcpdump` first: `sudo apt install tcpdump`

Now open a new Terminal tab/window and run: `sudo tcpdump -n -i any`

This process will stay running until you kill it with Ctrl+C or similar. Let it run for a bit just to see what kind of traffic it captures and to get a feel for the default output format. Depending on what's happening on your system, the output may scroll too quickly to read!

Kill that process with Ctrl+C and run something a bit more fine-tuned:

```
sudo tcpdump -n -i any -p icmp
```

This, of course, will only capture ICMP packets, a much more reasonable request. Now it's time to run some tests. Keep that process running, and in another tab or window, run: `ping -c 1 101labs.net`

If all goes well (you're not doing a lot of activity or running a router on your lab machine), `tcpdump` should show a clean output of two packets that looks (in part) something like this (the IP address may well differ if I move servers):

```
... IP 10.0.2.15 > 184.168.221.43: ICMP echo request ...
... IP 184.168.221.43 > 10.0.2.15: ICMP echo reply ...
```

It's easy to see what's happening here, but we've omitted some fields, and `tcpdump` has a lot of options to print a lot more fields. For example, if you change the ping's size by adding `-s 65507`, you may see something like:

```
... IP 10.0.2.15 > 184.168.221.43: ICMP echo request ... length 1480
... IP 10.0.2.15 > 184.168.221.43: ip-proto-1
... IP 10.0.2.15 > 184.168.221.43: ip-proto-1
... IP 10.0.2.15 > 184.168.221.43: ip-proto-1
... IP 10.0.2.15 > 184.168.221.43: ip-proto-1
... IP 10.0.2.15 > 184.168.221.43: ip-proto-1
... IP 10.0.2.15 > 184.168.221.43: ip-proto-1
```

This indicates that the packet has been fragmented. (It also happens that in this case the packet gets dropped or blocked somewhere, but that's not necessarily always the case.)

Other useful options include the `-w` switch to save packet captures to a file, and the `-c` switch to capture X number of packets instead of running forever.

Notes:
`tcpdump` is the classic packet monitor for Linux, but there are others, including Wireshark and `tshark`. Experiment to find your favorite.

LAB 70

Network Troubleshooting

Lab Objective:
Learn how to troubleshoot networking on a Linux host.

Lab Purpose:
In this lab, you will learn how to troubleshoot a Linux host as a network client, using various tools.

Lab Tool:
Ubuntu 18.04 (or another distro of your choice)

Lab Topology:
A single Linux machine, or virtual machine

Lab Walkthrough:

Task 1:
You've worked with `ip` in previous labs to get network information, but it's worth reiterating. It is a powerful tool with a lot of uses. Run the following commands now to get a feel for what kinds of information you can gather from it:

- `ip address`
- `ip maddress`
- `ip route`
- `ip netconf`

Task 2:
Install a couple of new tools: `sudo apt install iftop iperf`

`iftop` is a tool to monitor bandwidth usage, while `iperf` is a tool to test how much bandwidth you have (and, in the process, fills up enough for `iftop` to measure). Start `sudo iftop` in its own terminal tab/window and leave that running for now.

`iperf` requires a separate client and server to get any meaningful results. Fortunately, a number of public servers exist; visit **https://iperf.cc** to choose one near you, then run: `iperf -c [server] -p [port]`

While you're waiting, switch to the other tab to see what kind of bandwidth patterns are shown by `iftop`. When it's done, `iperf` will produce a report of your machine's bandwidth capabilities. Kill both processes before moving on.

Task 3:
`mtr` is a handy diagnostic tool that combines many of the uses of `ping` and `traceroute`. Its output is pretty self-explanatory: `mtr 101labs.net`

As this is an interactive program, type 'q' or Ctrl+C to quit.

Task 4:
Finally, install the venerable `whois`: `sudo apt install whois`

`whois` provides information about domain ownership and contact information. For example: `whois 101labs.net`

Often, but not always, the domain owner's contact information is hidden behind a registrar's privacy feature. What may be more useful, however, is the ability to discover an abuse contact in case of spam, phishing, or other nefarious activity originating from a domain.

This works on IP addresses as well: `whois 184.168.221.43`

Occasionally you may have need to discover the owners and abuse contacts behind an IP or block of IP's; this command will do that.

Notes:
Other networking tools were covered extensively in Labs 4-8.

LAB 71

Monitoring Disk Performance

Lab Objective:
Learn how to monitor the I/O performance of your storage devices.

Lab Purpose:
In this lab, you will use `ioping` and `iostat` to monitor disk I/O performance on your machine.

Lab Tool:
Ubuntu 18.04 (or another distro of your choice)

Lab Topology:
A single Linux machine, or virtual machine

Lab Walkthrough:

Task 1:
First, install a new performance monitoring tool: `sudo apt install ioping`

Then run `mkdir lab71` to prepare for the next step.

Compared with its cousin, `ping`, `ioping` measures the latency of disk I/O rather than the latency of a network connection. Run a few commands to compare the output. Each of these commands will run for ten seconds:

- `ioping -w 10 -A ./lab71`
- `ioping -w 10 -C ./lab71`
- `ioping -w 10 -L ./lab71`
- `ioping -w 10 -W ./lab71`
- `ioping -w 10 -R ./lab71    # No output until the end`

If you read the `man` page or run `ioping -h`, you will discover the meaning of each of those flags. The first test uses asynchronous I/O; the second takes advantage of caching; the third uses sequential operations (as opposed to random); the fourth uses write I/O (which can destroy a device if you aren't careful); the fifth runs a seek test.

Carefully compare the results of each test. Given what you know about disk operations under the hood, why do you think they are so different?

Finally, you can now `rmdir lab71`

Task 2:
Now run: `iostat -dh`

Depending on your machine, the output may show a long list of loopback devices (the lines beginning with "loop"). However, right now you are only interested in your main disk devices, of which there may be one or two, probably "sda," "sdb," or similar. The output will show five columns, indicating historical statistics of the indicated device: transfers per second, data written/read per second, and total data written/read.

For more information, add the `-x` flag (and read the `man` page to learn what all those abbreviations stand for!)

Notes:
Both `ioping` and `iostat` have modes for continually printing reports, so that you can monitor their output while performing another task. With `ioping`, simply omit the `-w` flag. With `iostat`, just add an interval at the end, like: `iostat -dh 5`

LAB 72

Monitoring Disk Usage

Lab Objective:
Learn how to monitor disk usage and free space.

Lab Purpose:
In this lab, you will use common Linux tools to monitor storage resources.

Lab Tool:
Ubuntu 18.04 (or another distro of your choice)

Lab Topology:
A single Linux machine, or virtual machine

Lab Walkthrough:

Task 1:
`df` is a tool commonly used to measure free space on a Linux disk or partition. Open the Terminal application and run: `df -h /dev/sd*`

This output should give you a listing of used and free space on your main partition (and any other disk partitions you may have).

`df` can also be used to calculate unused inodes: `df -hi /dev/sd*`

Typically—but not always—your inode usage, on a percentage basis, will be lower than your disk space usage.

Task 2:
In contrast to `df`, `du` is used to compute space (and inodes) allocated to one or more files or directories. A common use is like this: `du -h ~ | sort -h`

Can you figure out what's going on here? This command is recursively listing the contents of your home directory, sorted by their space usage. To show inodes instead, add the `--inodes` flag: `du -h --inodes ~ | sort -h`

Rather than a full recursive listing, you can also sum up the files/inodes in a given directory or set, like this:

- `du -hs ~`
- `du -hs --inodes ~`

Notes:
Labs 9-11 go into more details about disks, partitions, and filesystems.

LAB 73

CPU Configuration

Lab Objective:
Learn how to gather information about your CPU(s) and some configuration parameters.

Lab Purpose:
In this lab, you will use a few tools to learn about the CPU hardware of your lab machine and also how to configure some kernel parameters.

Lab Tool:
Ubuntu 18.04 (or another distro of your choice)

Lab Topology:
A single Linux machine, or virtual machine

Lab Walkthrough:

Task 1:
Open the Terminal appliation and run the following two commands:

- `lscpu`
- `cat /proc/cpuinfo`

You should see information about your CPU(s)—the hardware, not a virtualized CPU, if your hardware is at all modern. These two commands print mostly the same information, but in different ways. The former is more human-friendly, but the latter has some key tidbits, such as "bugs" which will tell you if your hardware is affected by, say, the recent Spectre or Meltdown vulnerabilities.

Task 2:
Now run: `sysctl -a |& grep -i cpu`

`sysctl` can be used to view or set a large number of kernel parameters. This command simply narrows that list to view the ones with "cpu" in the name, which... actually isn't all that helpful here. You can run `sudo sysctl -a`, if you dare, to view all 900+ parameters. However, you're probably most interested in the non-defaults: `sudo grep -rvh -e ^# -e ^$ /etc/sysctl{,.d/*}.conf`

It is impossible to predict what options might be set here, but on a default Ubuntu 18.04 system, you should have a few common options like:

```
net.ipv4.tcp_syncookies=1
net.ipv4.conf.all.rp_filter=1
```

These are both network security enhancements. You can view /etc/sysctl.conf and the files in /etc/sysctl.d to see comments on these options and why they are set the way they are. To change a setting yourself, you would add another .conf file to that directory and run: `sudo sysctl -p`

Notes:
In addition to using `sysctl`, a more ephemeral way (does not survive reboot) to change kernel parameters is to take advantage of the /proc filesystem. The details here are left as an exercise for the student.

LAB 74

CPU Monitoring

Lab Objective:
Learn how to monitor CPU usage and metrics.

Lab Purpose:
In this lab you will monitor CPU load and other metrics over time using a tool called `sar`.

Lab Tool:
Ubuntu 18.04 (or another distro of your choice)

Lab Topology:
A single Linux machine, or virtual machine

Lab Walkthrough:

Task 1:
If you don't already have `sysstat`, install it now: `sudo apt install sysstat`

NOTE: If `sysstat` was not previously installed, you should now give it at least 20-30 minutes to gather some data. This tool is most useful when it can collect data over a longer period of time.

Task 2:
Open a terminal and run `sar`

This is a basic output of some CPU metrics, listed by time period. "%user" here indicates the amount of CPU time spent on userspace tasks; "%system" indicates kernel space; "%iowait" indicates time waiting on disk (or perhaps network) I/O. "%steal" should be zero, except on busy virtual systems where the CPU may have to wait on another virtual CPU.

Not enough information for you? Well, you're in luck, because `sar` can do a lot more:

```
sar -qw -m CPU -u ALL -P ALL
```

The man pages explain a lot more, but this command will print information about queues, load averages, context switches, power management... basically everything you'd ever want to know about your CPU without getting into other hardware—and yes, `sar` can monitor that too!

Notes:

Many other tools, such as `top` or `uptime`, can show you a real-time view of CPU usage.

LAB 75

Swap Space

Lab Objective:
Learn how to configure swap space.

Lab Purpose:
Swap space is disk space used by the operating system when RAM is running low. In this lab, you will configure a swap file.

Lab Tool:
Ubuntu 18.04 (or another distro of your choice)

Lab Topology:
A single Linux machine, or virtual machine

Lab Walkthrough:

Task 1:
First, open the Terminal and run: `free -h`

Pay attention to the bottom line, labeled "Swap." Do you currently have a swap partition? Make note of the available swap space; you'll check it again later.

Task 2:
Now create and activate a 1GB swap file:

- `dd if=/dev/zero of=./lab75.img bs=1M count=1000`
- `mkswap ./lab75.img`
- `sudo swapon ./lab75.img`

You'll get some permissions warnings, but of course in this lab environment those can be safely ignored. Check `free -h` again, and you will see that your available swap space has grown by 1GB!

Task 3:

Finally, undo your previous steps to remove the insecure swap file:

- `sudo swapoff ./lab75.img`
- `rm lab75.img`

Notes:

Ideally, a healthy system rarely or never uses its swap space. Some Linux admins today prefer not to even set it up, but it is always nice to have some amount of swap space as a failsafe.

LAB 76

Memory Monitoring

Lab Objective:
Learn how to monitor memory usage on a Linux system.

Lab Purpose:
In this lab, you will explore monitoring memory usage and the OOM killer... and cause a bit of mayhem yourself.

Lab Tool:
Ubuntu 18.04 (or another distro of your choice)

Lab Topology:
A single Linux machine, or virtual machine

Lab Walkthrough:

Task 1:
Open the Terminal application with two tabs or windows.

In the first tab, run: `free -hs 0.5`

Keep that running for now. In the second tab:

```
a="a"; while true; do a+="$a"; done
```

Switch back to the first tab while that little one-liner causes all sorts of problems (as you will soon see). Do you notice your system's memory usage, and perhaps swap usage, climbing? Now go back to the second tab, observe what you typed, and see if you can understand why.

After several seconds, this tab should crash, out of a failure to find enough memory for its very hungry process.

Task 2:
Now Ctrl+C the `free` process, and instead run: `zgrep -i oom /var/log/kern*`

Ideally, this command should print... nothing! (Though if it did, that's fine, too.) What you're looking for here are messages from the kernel's OOM (out-of-memory) killer. You probably won't find any from the process you just ran, because that one was short-lived and basically self-limiting—as soon as the shell could no longer allocate memory, it terminated that process on its own.

The OOM killer runs when the kernel itself can't find enough memory to do its own tasks. If and when it does run, you will see logs in /var/log/kern*, among other places.

Notes:
You can use `vmstat` to serve a similar purpose to `free` (if a bit uglier). Finally, view the /proc/meminfo file for more than you ever wanted to know about your system's memory usage.

LAB 77

Resetting the Root Password

Lab Objective:
Learn how to reset a forgotten root password on Linux.

Lab Purpose:
In this lab, you will practice changing boot parameters for the purpose of resetting the root password.

Lab Tool:
Ubuntu 18.04 (or another distro of your choice)

Lab Topology:
A single Linux machine, or virtual machine

Lab Walkthrough:

IMPORTANT: This is one lab where the exact steps may vary greatly between distros, your particular bootloader configuration, and even different versions of Ubuntu. If you run into problems, Google may be enlightening.

Task 1:
Reboot until you reach the GRUB boot menu. If you cannot see the GRUB boot menu, follow Lab 2 and change your configuration so that you can.

Task 2:
Hit 'e' to edit the Ubuntu boot commands (should be the first menu item). Scroll down to the line beginning with `linux`. On that line, replace the `ro` option with `rw init=/bin/bash`, then hit Ctrl+X to boot.

Task 3:
You should boot into a root prompt with your root partition already mounted. Now simply run `passwd` to change the password, and then `reboot -f` to reboot.

Notes:

It is not possible to recover a lost disk encryption password (unless that password happens to be very weak). It is possible to recover a lost root password stored on an encrypted disk drive, but the steps are outside the scope of this lab.

LAB 78

Process Monitoring

Lab Objective:
Learn how to monitor processes and their resource usage.

Lab Purpose:
In this lab, you will learn how to monitor a number of metrics for both foreground and background processes.

Lab Tool:
Ubuntu 18.04 (or another distro of your choice)

Lab Topology:
A single Linux machine, or virtual machine

Lab Walkthrough:

Task 1:
If you weren't careful to terminate all of your sleep processes from Lab 48, you might have a stray or two running. Let's find out:

```
ps -ef
```

Well, that's a lot of output! You could maybe filter it through a `| grep sleep` or use `ps` without arguments, but there's a better way:

```
pgrep -a sleep
```

`pgrep` supports regex and has a number of matching options to make sure you find the right process(es).

Task 2:
A `sleep` process isn't going to use many system resources, but plenty of other processes might. It's important to know how to monitor those.

Take a look at `free -h`. This gives you an output of system memory usage. The most generally useful columns here are "total", "used", and "available." The "available" column offers an estimate of memory which is free for starting new processes without swapping. That isn't the same as "free" memory, which is often low on Linux systems. This is because the OS can take advantage of this memory for performance reasons, while still holding it as "available" for user processes.

`free` has a `-s N` switch to automatically print the output every N seconds. That's useful in its own right, but wouldn't you like to have that ability for every command? Then `watch` might be for you! `free -h -s 10` is equivalent to `watch -n 10 free -h`

Finally, take a look at the `top` command. Running `top` opens a rather confusing output screen that's continually changing, but one of its most useful capabilities may be simply sorting processes by CPU or memory usage. When in `top`, use the < and > keys to shift the sorting column over to the metric you're interested in. In the upper panel, you can also see the system load, a count of running processes, and some CPU and memory metrics. Finally, press 'q' to quit.

It is strongly recommended to spend some time reading the `top` man page, as this is one of the most featureful system monitoring tools that is installed by default.

Notes:

`uptime`, despite the name, is another quick way to get system load. However, `top` also shows this, as well as lots of other useful information.

LAB 79

Sending Signals

Lab Objective:
Learn how to send signals to processes in Linux.

Lab Purpose:
In this lab, you will learn about signals, including but not limited to kill, and how to send them to processes.

Lab Tool:
Ubuntu 18.04 (or another distro of your choice)

Lab Topology:
A single Linux machine, or virtual machine

Lab Walkthrough:

Task 1:
Sometimes, in Linux, things are not quite as they seem. This sequence of commands will demonstrate that:

- `sleep 10000 &`
- `kill -19 $(pgrep sleep)`
- `jobs`
- `kill -18 $(pgrep sleep)`
- `jobs`

What is happening here? Contrary to its name, the `kill` command doesn't necessarily kill processes. Instead, it sends them a *signal*, which may or may not be SIGKILL, the signal that immediately terminates a process. In fact, by default, `kill` doesn't even send SIGKILL—it sends SIGTERM (terminate gracefully), which is basically a computer's way of saying "please wrap up everything that you're doing... or else I'll have to send SIGKILL."

In this sequence, you first sent signal 19, which is SIGSTOP (stop), followed by signal 18, which is SIGCONT (continue). Given the output of `jobs`, this should now make more sense.

You can see a list of all signals with `kill -L`

Task 2:
Now create a few sleep processes if you haven't already, and use either `killall` or `pkill` to terminate them all with a single command. Both commands have the same general function, with slightly different arguments, so it's worth experimenting with and reading the man pages for both.

Notes:
`pkill` and `pgrep` have exactly the same searching/matching semantics. This means you can use `pgrep` as a "dry run" to find the processes you want to signal before actually doing so.

LAB 80

Modify Process Execution Priorities

Lab Objective:
Learn how to manage the priority of started and running processes.

Lab Purpose:
In this lab, you will learn how to get a running task's priority, change its priority, and set the priority of a task to be run.

Lab Tool:
Ubuntu 18.04 (or another distro of your choice)

Lab Topology:
A single Linux machine, or virtual machine

Lab Walkthrough:

Task 1:
Open the Terminal and run the following commands:

- `nice -n 19 sleep 10000 &`
- `ps -l`
- `sudo renice -n -20 $(pgrep sleep)`
- `ps -l`
- `pkill sleep`

What you've done here is started a `sleep` process with a "niceness" value of 19. This is the most "nice" a process can be—in other words, the least demanding in terms of priority. Then you changed its priority, with `renice`, to the "meanest" possible value of -20, or the most demanding in terms of priority. The default priority for all user processes is 0, and you must be root to run a process with higher priority. `ps -l` will list your running processes with their priorities.

Notes:
You can also use `top` to list and sort processes by their priority values.

LAB 81

Storage Quotas

Lab Objective:
Learn how to apply and enforce storage quotas.

Lab Purpose:
In this lab, you will experiment with applying storage quotas to users, and learn what happens when they are exceeded.

Lab Tool:
Ubuntu 18.04 (or another distro of your choice)

Lab Topology:
A single Linux machine, or virtual machine

Lab Walkthrough:

Task 1:
Install the quota package: `sudo apt install quota`

Now prepare the filesystem by remounting it with a couple of new options: `sudo mount -vo remount,usrjquota=aquota.user,jqfmt=vfsv1 /`

Finally, enable quotas:

- `sudo quotacheck -ucm /`
- `sudo quotaon -v /`

Task 2:
Now begin enabling a quota limit for your own user with: `sudo edquota $USER`

You should find yourself in an editor with some output looking like this:

```
Disk quotas for user ubuntu (uid 1000):
  Filesystem      blocks  soft     hard   inodes       soft    hard
  /dev/sda1       641072   0          0        19251           0   0
```

The block size here is 1Kb, so 641072 blocks means this user currently has roughly 641Mb worth of files. In the editor, change the first soft and hard numbers to be slightly more than the storage currently in use. In this example, we will use 645000 and 650000:

```
Disk quotas for user ubuntu (uid 1000):
  Filesystem       blocks  soft      hard     inodes          soft    hard
  /dev/sda1        641072    645000    650000        19251               0   0
```

Save and close the editor, then verify your own user's new quotas with: `quota`

Task 3:
Now run this (normally dangerous) command: `dd if=/dev/zero of=lab81`

Without quotas, this command would happily keep creating a useless file until your entire partition was full. With quotas enabled, `dd` will quit and print a "Disk quota exceeded" error in short order.

You can verify again with `quota`, and test to confirm that all file creation (and most modifications) by your user are now failing. As you might guess, disk quotas are critical in multi-user systems to prevent abuse.

Task 4:
Finally, undo the quotas and clean up:

- Run `sudo edquota $USER` again and undo your changes.
- `rm lab81`
- `sudo apt remove quota`

Notes:
Quotas can be enabled for groups as well. Simply add the mount option `grpjquota=aquota.group`. The options `usrquota/grpquota` will do non-journaled quotas, but you should use the journals if your file system supports them.

Depending upon your distro you may not be able to remount with:

```
sudo mount -vo remount,usrjquota=aquota.user,jqfmt=vfsv1 /
```

But the quota system works with just:

```
sudo mount -vo remount,usrjquota /dev/sdX /
```

LAB 82

Immutability

Lab Objective:
Learn about immutable files and directories, and their uses.

Lab Purpose:
In this lab you will use `chattr` to set and unset the immutability property, and understand what it means.

Lab Tool:
Ubuntu 18.04 (or another distro of your choice)

Lab Topology:
A single Linux machine, or virtual machine

Lab Walkthrough:

Task 1:
Create an example file: `echo hello > lab82.txt`

Add an immutable flag: `sudo chattr +i lab82.txt`

Now modify it: `echo goodbye > lab82.txt`

Hmm… did that not work? That's funny… can you delete it? `rm lab82.txt`

No? What about as root? `sudo rm lab82.txt`

Obviously, if you noted what the word "immutable" actually means, you understand what's going on here. You could use `lsattr [file]` to check whether a file has that flag—if so, the fifth field will be marked with `i`.

Task 2:

Now do a similar procedure for a directory:

- `mkdir lab82`
- `touch lab82/foo`
- `sudo chattr +i lab82`
- `touch lab82/bar`
- `rm lab82/foo`
- `rm -rf lab82`
- `lsattr -d lab82`

Immutability on directories works exactly as you would expect it to, with one interesting exception: It doesn't prevent the directory from acting as a mount point! This means you can mark the mount point for an external drive as immutable, which will prevent files from being written to it when that drive is not mounted.

Task 3:

Finally, clean up:

- `sudo chattr -i lab82*`
- `rm -rf lab82*`

Notes:

Some operating systems mark important binaries as immutable for security purposes, to make it more difficult for attackers to overwrite them with malicious versions.

LAB 83

Understanding Computer Hardware

Lab Objective:
Learn what hardware goes into building a computer and how to interface with some hardware from Linux.

Lab Purpose:
The following are primary hardware components in desktop and server computers:

- Motherboard
- Processor(s)
- Memory
- Power suppl(y/ies)
- Hard/solid-state disks
- Optical drives
- Peripherals

Lab Tool:
Ubuntu 18.04 (or another distro of your choice)

Lab Topology:
A single Linux machine, or virtual machine

Lab Walkthrough:

Task 1:
Open the Terminal and run the following commands to review some of the hardware (real or virtualized) which is powering your Linux computer:

- `lscpu`
- `lspci`
- `lsusb -t`
- `sudo lshw`
- `sudo hdparm -i /dev/sd*`

Task 2:

Now investigate some related low-level resources, like partitions, drivers (kernel modules), and resource usage:

- `sudo fdisk -l`
- `lsmod`
- `df -h`
- `free -m`

Notes:

If you want hardware information that you don't know how to find, a good way to start is by exploring the /proc filesystem. Most of the tools listed above simply gather and format information from /proc; that is where the kernel presents it.

LAB 84

RAID

Lab Objective:
Learn how to configure and manage software RAID configurations.

Lab Purpose:
A professional installation would create storage redundancy by using a hardware RAID device. In this lab, you will create "poor man's" redundancy by doing RAID in software, using `mdadm`.

Lab Tool:
Ubuntu 18.04 (or another distro of your choice)

Lab Topology:
A single Linux machine, or virtual machine

Lab Walkthrough:

Task 1:
First, install the RAID tools: `sudo apt install mdadm`

Now set up the virtual disks to be put into a RAID 1 array:

- `dd if=/dev/zero of=disk1.img bs=1M count=1000`
- `dd if=/dev/zero of=disk2.img bs=1M count=1000`
- `sudo losetup -fP disk1.img`
- `sudo losetup -fP disk2.img`
- `losetup -a | grep disk`

Make a note of the two devices printed at the beginning of each line produced by that last command. They should be files like /dev/loop18 and /dev/loop19, or similar. These will be noted as `[dev1]` and `[dev2]` in the commands below.

Task 2:

Create the array from the two loopback devices:

```
sudo mdadm -C /dev/md0 -l 1 -n 2 [dev1] [dev2]
```

The `-l` flag here designates the RAID level (in this case, level 1, a mirrored array). The `-n` flag specifies the number of disks in the array.

Verify that the array was created correctly with: `cat /proc/mdstat`

This file contains a list of arrays, their size, status, and the disks included in them, among other information.

Task 3:

After creating a filesystem on the array, you can use it like any other disk device:

- `sudo mkfs.ext4 /dev/md0`
- `mkdir lab84`
- `sudo mount /dev/md0 lab84`
- `sudo touch lab84/foo`

So what happens when one of the two disks fails? Let's simulate such a scenario now:

- `sudo mdadm -I -f [dev2]`
  NOTE: This command needs only a name for `[dev2]`, not a path. If the device is /dev/loop19, you would just use loop19.
- `cat /proc/mdstat`
- `sudo mdadm --detail /dev/md0`

You see here another way to get information about an array. This last command clearly lists one of the devices now as "removed" and the array's state as "clean, degraded".

Task 4:

Now you will repair this array, but there's no reason to make it simple...

- `sudo dd if=/dev/urandom of=lab84/bar`
- `sudo mdadm -a /dev/md0 [dev2] && sudo mdadm --detail /dev/md0`

In the first command, you're simply filling up the array with random data. The last two commands are combined into one, because you want to be able to see the array's status immediately after one of its disks is re-added.

Note now that your array is in "recovering" mode, that [dev2] is now rebuilding the data that it didn't have previously.

Task 5:
Finally, clean up:

- `sudo umount lab84`
- `sudo mdadm --stop /dev/md0`
- `sudo losetup -d [dev1]`
- `sudo losetup -d [dev2]`
- `rm disk{1,2}.img`

Notes:
There are several types of RAID configurations, not all of which provide any redundancy at all—RAID 0, for example, is meant for performance instead.

LAB 85

Patching

Lab Objective:
Learn how to apply software patches and update your system.

Lab Purpose:
In this lab, you will practice applying system updates and other software patches.

Lab Tool:
Ubuntu 18.04 (or another distro of your choice)

Lab Topology:
A single Linux machine, or virtual machine

Lab Walkthrough:

Task 1:
Apply system updates (on Ubuntu) with: `sudo apt full-upgrade`

If it's been a while since your last update, this may take some time, but in most cases that is all you need to do. In fact, that was so easy, why not automate it?

On a default system, the `unattended-upgrades` package should already be installed. If not, install it, then look at /etc/apt/apt.conf.d/50unattended-upgrades

It's worth noting that a typical configuration doesn't automatically apply *all* updates, just security patches. This is generally what you want.

To update a single package, simply run: `sudo apt upgrade [package]`

Labs 20-23 go into more detail on how to use various Linux package managers.

Notes:
You can apply source patches manually using the `patch` command. In practice, this is rarely done by non-developers, but can be useful if you are maintaining your own fork of some package.

LAB 86

Package Repositories

Lab Objective:
Learn how to configure package repositories (repos) for your system's package manager.

Lab Purpose:
In this lab, you will examine repo configurations and add a third-party repo to expand the selection of packages available to you.

Lab Tool:
Ubuntu 18.04 (or another distro of your choice)

Lab Topology:
A single Linux machine, or virtual machine

Lab Walkthrough:

Task 1:
Run `sudo apt edit-sources` to open the /etc/apt/sources.list file.

Here is a list of repos included with Ubuntu by default. Many are commented out, but now you will uncomment one and enable installation and updates from it. Scroll down and uncomment this line:

```
deb http://archive.canonical.com/ubuntu bionic partner
```

Save and quit the editor, then run `sudo apt update`

Task 2:
The Canonical partner repo contains a handful of tools that are not provided by Ubuntu, yet may be convenient. For example: `apt show adobe-flashplugin`

If you look at this output, particularly the APT-Sources line, you can see that the Adobe Flash plugin comes from the repo you just enabled.

Task 3:
Now you will add a repo that doesn't exist, for the purposes of seeing various ways that Apt can fail:

- `sudo apt edit-sources`
- At the bottom, add a new line:
  `deb http://example.com/badrepo bionic badrepo`
- `sudo apt update`

This first error message complains that your fake repo doesn't have a Release file. This is not a mistake that any actual maintainer would make, so for now, just work around it:

- `sudo apt edit-sources`
- In the bottom line, immediately after `deb`, add: `[allow-insecure=yes]`
- `sudo apt update`

The Release file error has now been converted to a warning, and now Apt is complaining that it can't find necessary index files which should be included in the repo. Naturally, this requires a repo that actually functions.

Despite this problem, actions related to other repos will still work—although you may see some warnings clogging your output.

Task 4:
Clean up:

- `sudo apt edit-sources`
- Delete the last line
- Comment out the Canonical partner line (unless you want to keep it)
- Save and quit, then `sudo apt update`

Notes:
Adding third-party repos can be a security risk, so always make sure to only use trustworthy ones. RPMFusion is an example of a popular third-party repo for RedHat-based distros.

LAB 87

Memory Testing

Lab Objective:
Learn how to test your system RAM hardware for problems.

Lab Purpose:
In this lab, you will learn about two tools that can be used to test system RAM.

Lab Tool:
Ubuntu 18.04 (or another distro of your choice)

Lab Topology:
A single Linux machine, or virtual machine

Lab Walkthrough:

Task 1:
Install `memtester`: `sudo apt install memtester`

This is a tool can which can test memory while your operating system is running. First, use `free -m` to figure out how much memory your system has. Unless you suspect actual problems, you should be conservative here and test no more than 50% of your RAM. Pass this to `memtester` as a number of MB, followed by a number of iterations. For example, if you want to run a single test of 1024MB, run:

```
sudo memtester 1024 1
```

This will take some time, but in the end you will be presented with a (hopefully clean) report.

Task 2:
Now reboot your system to the GRUB menu and select `memtest86+`. This is a Linux package, installed with Ubuntu by default, but run through GRUB. It works in a similar way to `memtester`, running a variety of tests over a number of iterations. However,

because it cannot have the OS interfering with its operations, it is arguably more accurate.

Notes:
Genuine memory problems are hard to diagnose except by trial and error. This is because problems with other hardware, such as CPU, PSU, or motherboard, can manifest as memory errors in some tests.

Automation and Scripting

LAB 88

Shell Scripting

Lab Objective:
Learn how to write a simple shell script containing multiple commands.

Lab Purpose:
Scripting with Bash is a daily task by many professional Linux administrators. When a task is repetitive, you don't want to be typing the same list of commands over and over; you want to create a script, and perhaps also schedule that script to run automatically.

Lab Tool:
Ubuntu 18.04 (or another distro of your choice)

Lab Topology:
A single Linux machine, or virtual machine

Lab Walkthrough:

Task 1:
Open the Terminal application, and run your favorite text editor, such as `vi` or `nano`. (If you have never used `vi` or `vim`, then `nano` is strongly recommended.)

Create a file with the following contents:

```
#!/bin/bash
for (( n=0; n<$1; n++ ))
do
  echo $n
done
echo "Output from $0 complete."
```

Task 2:
Make the file executable (with `chmod +x filename`), then run it like:

```
./filename 10
```

You should see the numbers 0-9 printed out, one at a time. Knowing what the script does now, can you understand it in its entirety? What happens if you fail to pass an argument, or if you pass "gibberish," like letters instead of a number?

Task 3:

Run your script without an argument. Then run: `echo $?`

`$?` is a special variable that references the *exit status*. In a successful program, the exit status would be 0. Please try it for yourself now. Then edit the script by removing the last echo statement. This script then fails without an argument, returning a different exit status.

Notes:

That first line, starting with `#!` (called a *shebang*), denotes what program will be used to interpret your script. Usually, this is `/bin/bash`, but it can also be another shell like `/bin/zsh`, or even another programming language like `/usr/bin/python`.

In this case, you could remove the shebang line, because your interpreter is the same (Bash) as the shell you are currently running. But you should always include it because you never know when you might want to share a script with someone using a different shell.

LAB 89

Environment Variables, Types, and History

Lab Objective:
Learn about Bash environment variables, types, and how to use the shell history.

Lab Purpose:
The Bash command shell is pre-installed on millions of Linux computers around the world. Understanding how this shell works is a critical skill for working with Linux.

Lab Tool:
Ubuntu 18.04 (or another distro of your choice)

Lab Topology:
A single Linux machine, or virtual machine

Lab Walkthrough:

Task 1:
Open the Terminal application, then enter: `echo $PATH`

The PATH environment variable lists all locations that Bash will search when you enter a command with a *relative* path. A *relative* path example is `bash`, compared to `/bin/bash`, which is an *absolute* path.

There are other environment variables as well. You can view all of them, and their values, using the `env` command.

Task 2:
You can add or modify an environment variable with `export`. For example:

```
export PATH=${PATH}:./
```

In most cases this change will disappear when you exit Bash, but the advantage of `export` is that child processes will now be able to see the new/modified variable.

For example:

- `foo=123`
- `export bar=456`
- `bash`
- `echo $foo $bar`

This prints `456`, because only `bar` is seen by the child shell.

Task 3:
Another useful Bash command is called `type`. Use `type` to figure out information on other commands or functions:

```
type -a date
type -a if
type -a echo
type -a ls
```

`type` will tell you if a command/shell function is a binary file (like /bin/date), a shell built-in (like `help`), an alias (which you can view with `alias`), or a shell keyword (like `if` or `while`).

Task 4:
Enter `history` to see a history of commands you have typed into Bash.

To repeat a command, simply enter `!` and then the appropriate number. For example. `!12` will execute command #12 in the history list.

If you accidentally saved a password or other sensitive information to the history, you may use, for example, `history -d 47` to delete command #47 from the list, or even `history -c` to clear the history altogether.

If you want to save your current shell's history to another file, use `history -w filename`

The default filename Bash saves its history to is .bash_history. However, by default it only saves at the end of a session. If your session crashes, or you open multiple sessions, etc., then your shell history could become incomplete or out of order.

Notes:
If you wish to permanently modify an environment variable or other shell settings, look into the `.bashrc` and `.bash_profile` files.

LAB 90

Standard Syntax

Lab Objective:
Learn about standard shell syntax specific to scripting setup.

Lab Purpose:
In this lab, you will learn about standard shell scripting syntax, such as tests and control flow.

Lab Tool:
Ubuntu 18.04 (or another distro of your choice)

Lab Topology:
A single Linux machine, or virtual machine

Lab Walkthrough:

Task 1:
Open your favorite editor via the terminal and create a file called lab66.sh:

```
#!/bin/sh

i=0
while test $i -lt 5
do
  echo $i
  i=$(($i+1))
done

for file in $(ls /etc)
do
  test -r /etc/$file && echo "$file is readable by $USER."
  test -s /etc/$file || echo "$file has size zero!"
  if test -d /etc/$file
  then
    echo "$file is a directory."
  fi
done
```

This highly contrived and not very useful script contains a number of important features. The first is `test`, which can test a wide variety of conditions depending on its flags and return a 0 or 1 (true or false) exit status. That exit status can, in turn, be used by control flow syntax—`if` statements, or `for` or `while` loops. A simpler kind of `if` statement is the `&&` or `||` syntax, a boolean 'and' or 'or', respectively.

If you wish, you can test the script by executing it with:

- `chmod +x lab66.sh`
- `./lab66.sh`

You should see the numbers 0-4 printed out, followed by a large amount of text output, depending on what's in your /etc directory.

Notes:
This is a somewhat-rare situation where using /bin/sh and /bin/bash as the interpreter may yield different results. Bash has a `((++var))` syntax for variable incrementation, which is non-standard in the normal Bourne shell. Similar for `[[ ]]` (a test syntax) and the C-style for loop syntax: `for ((i=0; i<5; i++))...`

LAB 91

Quoting and Escaping

Lab Objective:
Learn basic Linux commands and shell syntax.

Lab Purpose:
The Bash command shell is pre-installed on millions of Linux computers around the world. Understanding how this shell works is a critical skill for working with Linux.

Lab Tool:
Ubuntu 18.04 (or another distro of your choice)

Lab Topology:
A single Linux machine, or virtual machine

Lab Walkthrough:

Task 1:
Open the Terminal application, then enter: `echo Hello World`

The `echo` command simply prints out all of the "words," or arguments, that you give to it. This might not seem very useful, until...

Task 2:
Now enter the following four commands, in order:

```
quote='cat /etc/issue'
backquote=`cat /etc/issue`
echo $quote
echo $backquote
```

Here, `quote` and backquote are called *variables.* In the first two lines, we set them to the values `'cat /etc/issue'` and `` `cat /etc/issue` ``, respectively. (We'll get to the difference between quotes and backquotes in a minute.) In the last two lines, we reference the variables by putting `$` before them, and print out their contents.

Task 3:

To understand single quotes, double quotes, and backquotes, enter the following:

```
hello="echo hello"
echo "$hello"
echo '$hello'
echo `$hello`
```

Double quotes allow for variables to have their values referenced. Single quotes are always literal, while backquotes *execute* the command (including variable references) within those quotes.

Task 4:

Sometimes you will need to distinguish certain characters on the command line, using what is called *escaping*. Try the following command sequence:

- `echo hello > foo bar`
- `cat foo bar`

Your output should be:

```
hello bar
cat: bar: No such file or directory
```

What's going on here? Both `echo` and `cat` are interpreting the space between `foo` and `bar` to indicate separate arguments rather than a single filename, as intended. You could put 'foo bar' into quotes, or you could escape the space by using a backslash, as follows:

- `echo hello > foo\ bar`
- `cat foo\ bar`

It is safe to assume that any character which may be interpreted directly by the shell, when your intention is for it to be part of an argument, should be escaped. Examples include but are not limited to: whitespace, >, <, $, *, &, and quotes.

Notes:

In some cases, you will want to reference variables with the `${variable}` syntax. This is equivalent to `$variable`, but the reasons for choosing one over the other are beyond the scope of this lab.

Backquotes also have an alternative syntax:

```
$(echo hello)
```

This syntax is generally preferred over backquotes. We only mention backquotes to distinguish them from single quotes and ensure the differences are clear.

LAB 92

Regular Expressions

Lab Objective:
Learn how to use regular expressions for complex string pattern matching.

Lab Purpose:
Regular expressions are a tool used commonly in Linux to match complex patterns in strings and text files. Many tools support regular expressions.

Lab Tool:
Ubuntu 18.04 (or another distro of your choice)

Lab Topology:
A single Linux machine, or virtual machine

Lab Walkthrough:

Task 1:
Open the Terminal application. See if you can predict what the output of this command sequence will be before you run it (see **Answer 1** below):

```
echo "foo
bar
baz
quux
frob
plugh
xyzzy" | sort | tail -5 | grep [be]
```

Task 2:

Can you match which of the following strings (on the right) would match each regular expression (on the left)? Each regex may have multiple matches! See **Answer 2** below for the solution.

`^s?.*$`	`Hello World`
`^[0-9] .*$`	`1, 2, 3, Go!`
`^.*[a-z].*$`	`sayonara`
`^q?[a-z]*$`	`101labs`

Answer 1:

```
frob
```

Answer 2:

The first expression matches all four strings.
The second expression matches "1, 2, 3, Go!" and "101labs".
The third expression matches all four strings.
The fourth expression matches "sayonara".

Notes:

Regexr is a great resource for practicing your regular expressions.

LAB 93

Basic Regex

Lab Objective:
Learn how to use basic regular expressions for complex string pattern matching.

Lab Purpose:
Regular expressions are a tool used commonly in Linux to match complex patterns in strings and text files. Many tools support regular expressions. With basic regex, some metacharacters require backslashes in front of them.

Lab Tool:
Ubuntu 18.04 (or another distro of your choice)

Lab Topology:
A single Linux machine, or virtual machine

Lab Walkthrough:

Task 1:
Open the Terminal application and create a text file first (copy and paste won't work for the below):

```
echo “abc123
456def
<html>
Hello World!
password
01234567890
A1B2C3D4E5
6F7G8H9I0J
Quoth the raven: ‘Nevermore.’” > lab93.txt
```

Task 2:

Now, try to predict what the output of each command will be before running it (see **Answers 1-7** below):

- `grep [0-3] lab93.txt`
- `grep [e68] lab93.txt`
- `grep "^[0-9a-zA-Z]\+$" lab93.txt`
- `grep "[0-9][A-Z]\?[0-9]" lab93.txt`
- `grep "<\|:" lab93.txt`
- `grep -v ".*" lab93.txt`
- `fgrep -v ".*" lab93.txt`

That last command is a bit of a curveball. `fgrep` (short for `grep -F`) treats an expression as a literal string and does not use regex matching. So it is excluding all matches containing a literal '.*'—which, of course, is none of them.

Answer 1:

```
abc123
01234567890
A1B2C3D4E5
6F7G8H9I0J
```

Answer 2:

```
456def
Hello World!
01234567890
6F7G8H9I0J
Quoth the raven: 'Nevermore.'
```

Answer 3:

```
abc123
456def
password
01234567890
A1B2C3D4E5
6F7G8H9I0J
```

Answer 4:

```
abc123
456def
01234567890
A1B2C3D4E5
6F7G8H9I0J
```

Answer 5:

```
<html>
Quoth the raven: 'Nevermore.'
```

Answer 6:

(No output)

Answer 7:

```
abc123
456def
<html>
Hello World!
password
01234567890
A1B2C3D4E5
6F7G8H9I0J
Quoth the raven: 'Nevermore.'
```

Notes:
Regexr is a great resource for practicing your regular expressions. See `man 7 regex` for more information on regex as supported by your distro.

LAB 94

Extended Regex

Lab Objective:
Learn how to use extended regular expressions for complex string pattern matching.

Lab Purpose:
Regular expressions are a tool used commonly in Linux to match complex patterns in strings and text files. Many tools support regular expressions. With extended regex, metacharacters do not require backslashes.

Lab Tool:
Ubuntu 18.04 (or another distro of your choice)

Lab Topology:
A single Linux machine, or virtual machine

Lab Walkthrough:

Task 1:
Open the Terminal application and create a text file first:

```
echo "abc123
456def
<html>
Hello World!
password
01234567890
A1B2C3D4E5
6F7G8H9I0J
Quoth the raven: 'Nevermore.'" > lab94.txt
```

Task 2:
Now, try to predict what the output of each command will be before running it (see **Answers 1-7** below):

- egrep [0-3] lab94.txt
- egrep [e68] lab94.txt
- egrep “^[0-9a-zA-Z]+$” lab94.txt
- egrep “[0-9][A-Z]?[0-9]” lab94.txt
- egrep “<|:” lab94.txt
- egrep -v “.*” lab94.txt
- egrep “[ls]{2}” lab94.txt

egrep (short for grep -E) uses extended regex, instead of basic regex, which is the default.

Task 3:
Finally, apply some of what you've learned about regex to these sed substitution commands. Again, what will the output be (see **Answers 8-10** below)?

- sed -E ‘s/[A-Z]/_/g’ lab94.txt
- sed -E ‘s/^[a-z]+$/[omitted]/’ lab94.txt
- sed -E ‘s/([a-z])\1/**/g’ lab94.txt

Answer 1:

```
abc123
01234567890
A1B2C3D4E5
6F7G8H9I0J
```

Answer 2:

```
456def
Hello World!
01234567890
6F7G8H9I0J
Quoth the raven: ‘Nevermore.’
```

Answer 3:

```
abc123
456def
password
01234567890
A1B2C3D4E5
6F7G8H9I0J
```

Answer 4:

```
abc123
456def
01234567890
A1B2C3D4E5
6F7G8H9I0J
```

Answer 5:

```
<html>
Quoth the raven: 'Nevermore.'
```

Answer 6:

(No output)

Answer 7:

```
Hello World!
password
```

Answer 8:

```
abc123
456def
<html>
_ello _orld!
password
01234567890
_1_2_3_4_5
6_7_8_9_0_
_uoth the raven: '_evermore.'
```

Answer 9:

```
abc123
456def
<html>
Hello World!
[omitted]
01234567890
A1B2C3D4E5
6F7G8H9I0J
Quoth the raven: 'Nevermore.'
```

Answer 10:

```
abc123
456def
<html>
He**o World!
pa**word
01234567890
A1B2C3D4E5
6F7G8H9I0J
Quoth the raven: 'Nevermore.'
```

Notes:

Regexr is a great resource for practicing your regular expressions. See `man 7 regex` for more information on regex as supported by your distro.

LAB 95

Scripting Practice

Lab Objective:
Use what you already know to write a simple shell script, from scratch.

Lab Purpose:
Scripting with Bash is a daily task by many professional Linux administrators. When a task is repetitive, you don't want to be typing the same list of commands over and over; you want to create a script, and perhaps also schedule that script to run automatically.

Lab Tool:
Ubuntu 18.04 (or another distro of your choice)

Lab Topology:
A single Linux machine, or virtual machine

Lab Walkthrough:

Task 1:
Open the Terminal application, and run your favorite text editor, such as `vi` or `nano`. (If you have never used `vi` or `vim`, then `nano` is strongly recommended.)

You may wish to reference Lab 15 if you have not already done so. Your goal is to write a script which accepts one argument—a number—and prints out two numbers at a time such that:

- The first number counts down from the argument to 0
- The second number counts up from 0 to the argument

Example:

```
./foo.sh 100
100 0
99 1
98 2
...
```

If the user doesn't pass an argument, or passes an argument that doesn't make sense, like a word, you should print a friendly message like "Please give a number."

Remember to make the file executable (with `chmod +x filename`) before testing it. See **Answer 1** below for one possible solution.

Answer 1:

```
#!/bin/bash
if ! [ "$1" -ge 0 ]
then
  echo "Please give a number."
  exit 1
fi
for (( n=0; n<=$1; n++ ))
do
  echo $(($1-$n)) $n
done
```

Notes:
In Lab 15, you read about the exit status. For error-checking purposes: Can you figure out how to use the exit status before your script has exited?

LAB 96

Scripting Practice 2

Lab Objective:
Use what you already know to write a simple shell script, from scratch.

Lab Purpose:
Scripting with Bash is a daily task by many professional Linux administrators. When a task is repetitive, you don't want to be typing the same list of commands over and over; you want to create a script, and perhaps also schedule that script to run automatically.

Lab Tool:
Ubuntu 18.04 (or another distro of your choice)

Lab Topology:
A single Linux machine, or virtual machine

Lab Walkthrough:

Task 1:
Open the Terminal application and run your favorite text editor.

You may wish to reference Labs 66 and 67 if you have not already done so. Your goal is to write a script which accepts three arguments—a directory path, and two flags to be passed to `test`. This script should check every file in the directory (non-recursively) and, if it passes *both* tests, prints that file's name.

Example:

```
./foo.sh ~/mydir -f -w
myfile
```

In this example, the script is looking for files with ~/mydir that are regular files with write permissions granted. myfile passes those tests.

All error conditions should print a friendly message and exit with status 1. For example, if three arguments are not passed, or the passed directory doesn't exist, or one of the `test` arguments is not valid. See **Answer 1** below for one possible solution.

For an extra challenge, you might print all files, but sort them according to how many tests they passed.

Answer 1:

```
#!/bin/bash

test $# -eq 3 || { echo "Exactly three arguments are required."; exit
1; }
test -d $1 || { echo "Not a directory."; exit 1; }
files=$(ls $1 2>/dev/null) || { echo "I can't read that directory.";
exit 1; }

for f in $files; do
  test $2 $1/$f 2>/dev/null
  rc1=$?
  test $3 $1/$f 2>/dev/null
  rc2=$?
  test $rc1 -gt 1 && { echo "First test argument is invalid."; exit 1; }
  test $rc2 -gt 1 && { echo "Second test argument is invalid."; exit 1; }
  test $rc1 -eq 0 && test $rc2 -eq 0 && echo $f
done
```

Notes:
Remember that using /bin/sh as an interpreter can have different results from /bin/bash! It is good to understand what makes a *Bourne-compatible* shell, and what non-Bourne-compatible additions are available in Bash.

LAB 97

Creating a Git Repo

Lab Objective:
Learn how to create a repository in Git, a popular version control tool.

Lab Purpose:
In this lab, you will create a Git repo to serve as a basis from which to learn other Git operations in Labs 98 and 99.

Lab Tool:
Ubuntu 18.04 (or another distro of your choice)

Lab Topology:
A single Linux machine, or virtual machine

Lab Walkthrough:

Task 1:
Install Git, if you haven't already: `sudo apt install git`

Create a new directory with some simple files to start with:

- `mkdir myrepo`
- `cd myrepo`
- `echo 'Hello World!' > hello.txt`
- `echo 'This is a very important file. Do not delete.' > README`

Now, to initialize the repo, just run: `git init`

Task 2:
If you've never used Git on this system before, then you probably haven't added your name and e-mail address yet. This isn't a website signup form, but a configuration file which tells other collaborators who committed a given piece of code. Run `git config --global -e`, edit the file with your name and e-mail, then save and quit.

You can also use `git config -e` to edit the local (repo-specific) configuration file, which is located at .git/config, but you don't need to worry about that right now.

What you may want to do now is edit the .git/description file which, as you might guess, is a description of the repo.

Notes:
Most Git repos include a .gitignore file, which tells Git to ignore certain types of files in the directory and not include them as part of the repo. There are many .gitignore templates available, which vary based on what programming language(s) or other data is included in the repo.

LAB 98

Working with Git

Lab Objective:
Learn how to use basic day-to-day Git operations for version control.

Lab Purpose:
In this lab, you will practice working with `commit` and other operations for managing code collaboration in Git.

Lab Tool:
Ubuntu 18.04 (or another distro of your choice)

Lab Topology:
A single Linux machine, or virtual machine

Lab Walkthrough:

Task 1:
First, you will need a Git repo. If you don't have one, you may reference Lab 97, or find an interesting repo on the internet and use `git clone` to retrieve it. This lab will assume you are using the repo from Lab 97.

Task 2:
Make sure your working directory is the repo's directory, e.g. ~/myrepo. At this point, you have a repo, but should not have made any commits yet. Run the following commands to fix that:

- `git add hello.txt README`
- `git commit -am "Initial commit"`

You can see your commit with `git log`. To make further changes, follow the same workflow: Edit any files that need editing, and run `git commit` again.

It's important to note that, in a typical development setting, you would usually do one more step after you were done making commits: `git push`. This pushes your most recent commits to a remote repo, which is often, but not always, a central server from which the rest of your team can pick up the changes.

To pick up changes made by your teammates, you would use `git pull`.

Notes:
You can use `git show` to show exactly what changes were made by a given commit. The syntax is `git show [hash]`, where `[hash]` is the hash shown in git log. Or, alternatively, just `git show` to show the most recent commit.

LAB 99

Git Branches

Lab Objective:
Learn how to work with branches in Git.

Lab Purpose:
In this lab, you will practice using `branch` and `merge` operations for advanced code collaboration in Git.

Lab Tool:
Ubuntu 18.04 (or another distro of your choice)

Lab Topology:
A single Linux machine, or virtual machine

Lab Walkthrough:

Task 1:
First, you will need a Git repo. If you don't have one, you may reference Lab 97, or find an interesting repo on the internet and use `git clone` to retrieve it. This lab will assume you are using the repo from Lab 97.

Task 2:
The default code branch in Git is called `master`. Sometimes you want to "branch off" and work on a large block of code without interfering with `master`, maybe for the purposes of experimenting. Make sure your working directory is the repo's directory, then do that now with: `git checkout -b lab99`

This is a shortcut for just creating a branch and then checking it out at the same time. You can confirm that you are now using the lab99 branch with: `git branch`

Task 3:
Now, safely on the lab99 branch, make a few modifications:

- `echo 'I love git branches!' > lab99.txt`
- `git add lab99.txt`
- `git commit -am "Lab 99"`

Unfortunately, there's been a problem. While you were playing around with this lab, a critical security patch was applied to the `master` branch:

- `git checkout master`
- `echo 'This file is obsolete and should be removed.' > README`
- `git commit -am "Bug fix #42"`

Task 4:
Now, you may notice, the two branches are out of sync. Each branch has a commit that the other one doesn't. That's where `git merge` comes into play:

- `git checkout lab99`
- `git merge master`

Using `cat README`, you can confirm that the patch from `master` was applied to `lab99`.

Finally, you can merge `lab99` back into `master` and remove the branch:

- `echo 'And merging, too!' >> lab99.txt`
- `git commit -am "I <3 merging"`
- `git checkout master`
- `git merge lab99`
- `git branch -d lab99`

Notes:
One important case not covered here was merge conflicts, i.e. what happens when two changes conflict within a merge. Typically Git will warn you and indicate the conflict within one or more files, which you can then examine with `git diff` (and an editor).

LAB 100

Ansible

Lab Objective:
Learn how to use the Ansible configuration management tool.

Lab Purpose:
In this lab, you will practice using Ansible, which is an infrastructure automation tool to make lives easier for professional system administrators.

Lab Tool:
Ubuntu 18.04 (or another distro of your choice)

Lab Topology:
A single Linux machine, or virtual machine

Lab Walkthrough:

Task 1:
First, install Ansible:

- `sudo apt-add-repository --yes --update ppa:ansible/ansible`
- `sudo apt install ansible`

Add your localhost to the Ansible hosts file, telling it that your local machine is one of the devices (in this case, the only device) it should manage:

```
sudo sh -c 'echo localhost >> /etc/ansible/hosts'
```

Ansible connects over SSH, so normally you would need to do a bit of setup to ensure that SSH connectivity is working. On localhost, you should be able to skip this step. Use `ansible -m ping all` to confirm that Ansible can connect; the result should look something like this:

```
localhost | SUCCESS => {
    "changed": false,
    "ping": "pong"
}
```

Task 2:

To run a one-off shell command on all Ansible hosts, try something like:

```
ansible -m shell -a 'free -m' all
```

This is a useful feature, but not nearly the most useful. Open your favorite editor and create an Ansible playbook file called lab100.yml, with the following text:

```
---
- hosts: all
  tasks:
     - name: hello
       copy: src=hello.txt dest=~/lab100.txt
```

And of course you must create the hello.txt file to copy:

```
echo 'Hello World!' > hello.txt
```

Now run: `ansible-playbook lab100.yml`

And the lab100.txt file will now exist in your home directory. Running the same `ansible-playbook` command will show no changes; removing lab100.txt and running it again will cause the file to be recreated. Modifying the file and running it will cause your changes to be reverted.

Can you understand how Ansible is useful for managing hundreds or thousands of devices?

Notes:

This is only one very small example usage of a complex and powerful tool. Ansible is well worth understanding if you aspire to manage Linux machines professionally.

LAB 101

Puppet

Lab Objective:
Learn how to use the Puppet configuration management tool.

Lab Purpose:
In this lab, you will practice using Puppet, which is an infrastructure automation tool to make lives easier for professional system administrators.

Lab Tool:
Ubuntu 18.04 (or another distro of your choice)

Lab Topology:
A single Linux machine, or virtual machine

Lab Walkthrough:

Task 1:
First, install Puppet: `sudo apt install puppet puppetmaster`

Unlike Ansible's default setup (see Lab 100), Puppet uses a client-server model with a "puppetmaster" server from which nodes pull their manifests. Thus, in a production environment, you would set up this puppetmaster server and install the Puppet client on each node you want to manage.

Some configuration:

- `sudo puppet config set server localhost`
- `sudo puppet config set certname localhost`
- `sudo puppet agent -t`
- `sudo puppet ca sign localhost`
- `sudo systemctl restart puppetmaster`
- `sudo systemctl start puppet`

This is a somewhat non-trivial process to get both the Puppet client and server talking to each other on the same machine. In a typical installation, you would follow mostly the same steps, by requesting a certificate from the client and then signing it from the server.

Task 2:

Now the fun begins. Open an editor, as root, and create /etc/puppet/code/site.pp with the following contents:

```
node default {
  file { '/tmp/lab101.txt':
    content => 'Hello World!',
  }
}
```

In a typical environment, you'd have a more complex directory structure with multiple modules and environments, and the Puppet agents would automatically pick up changes every 30 minutes. Since this is a lab environment and the directory structures aren't fully set up (and you don't want to wait 30 minutes anyway), just apply this manifest as a one-off:

```
sudo puppet apply site.pp
```

The lab101.txt file will now exist in /tmp. Running the same command again will show no changes; removing lab101.txt and running it again will cause the file to be recreated. Modifying the file and running it will cause your changes to be reverted.

Can you understand how Puppet is useful for managing hundreds or thousands of devices?

Notes:

This is only one very small example usage of a complex and powerful tool. Puppet is well worth understanding if you aspire to manage Linux machines professionally.

Made in United States
Orlando, FL
04 November 2026

90206057R00146